Working Words in
SPELLING

G. Willard Woodruff and George N. Moore
with Robert G. Forest • Richard A. Talbot • Ann R. Talbot

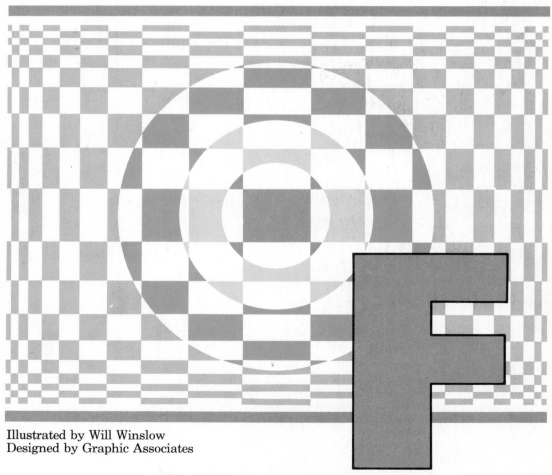

Illustrated by Will Winslow
Designed by Graphic Associates

D.C. Heath and Company
Lexington, Massachusetts/Toronto, Canada

Become a S-H-A-R-P Speller

See the word.
- Look at the word.
- Think about the letters that spell the word.

Hear the word.
- Say the word.
- Listen to the consonant and vowel sounds.

Adopt the word.
- Close your eyes.
- See the word in your mind's eye.
- Think about how it looks and sounds.

Record the word.
- Cover the word.
- Write the word.

Proofread the word.
- Correct the word.
- Touch each letter.
- Think about the word again.

SPELLEX®—a registered trademark of Curriculum Associates, Inc.
SPELLEX® Glossary incorporated by permission of Curriculum Associates, Inc.
Handwriting models in this book are reproduced with permission of Zaner-Bloser, Inc., from the series *HANDWRITING: Basic Skills and Application,* ©1984.
Copyright ©1988 by D.C. Heath and Company

Published simultaneously in Canada
Printed in the United States of America
International Standard Book Number: 0-669-15459-8
1 2 3 4 5 6 7 8 9 0

Lesson 1

I. Check Test. Write each spelling word.

II. Spelling Words and Phrases

spade	will **spade** the garden
salesperson	**salesperson** at the door
pavement	cracks in the **pavement**
behave	should **behave** better
locate	will try to **locate** it
grateful	**grateful** for the favor
debate	an angry **debate**
rating	were **rating** their work
estate	a huge private **estate**
haste	too much **haste**
bathe	will **bathe** with warm water
ache	a constant **ache**
headache	cured my **headache**
calendar	a school **calendar**
vanish	to **vanish** without a sign
sandwich	peanut butter **sandwich**
anxious	was very **anxious**
champion	want to be **champion**
establish	to **establish** a colony
disaster	to avoid **disaster**

III. Find a Fit. Write each word in its correct shape.

a.
b.
c.
d.
e.
f.
g.
h.
i.
j.
k.
l.
m.
n.
o.
p.
q.
r.
s.
t.

Other Word Forms

spaded, spading, salespeople, pave, paving, behaves, behaving, behavior, locates, locating, location, gratefully, debated, debating, debater, rate, rated, ratings, estates, hastily, bathes, bathed, bathing, ached, aching, headaches, calendars, vanishes, vanished, vanishing, sandwiches, sandwiched, anxiously, championship, establishes, established, establishment, disastrous

IV. Break the Code. Use the code to write the spelling words.

a	b	c	d	e	f	g	h	i	j	k	l	m	n	o	p	q	r	s	t	u	v	w	x	y	z
↓	↓	↓	↓	↓	↓	↓	↓	↓	↓	↓	↓	↓	↓	↓	↓	↓	↓	↓	↓	↓	↓	↓	↓	↓	↓
p	e	g	s	v	k	x	m	c	f	h	t	i	u	r	b	a	o	q	d	z	n	l	y	w	j

a. qikb _____

b. eqvmdk _____

c. pbkqeb _____

d. daqtb _____

e. bdlqpwmdk _____

f. coqlbjnw _____

g. oqlmvc _____

h. qvgmrnd _____

i. kqdlb _____

j. dqwbdabodrv _____

k. wriqlb _____

l. tmdqdlbo _____

m. kbqtqikb _____

n. dqvtymik _____

o. tbpqlb _____

p. aqebhbvl _____

q. iqwbvtqo _____

r. bdlqlb _____

s. ikqhamrv _____

t. pqlkb _____

V. Generally Speaking. Write each spelling word in the group it best fits.

a. control oneself, act, _____

b. argue, dispute, _____

c. appreciative, thankful, _____

d. sidewalk, concrete, _____

e. set up, arrange, _____

f. date, appointment book, _____

g. winner, the best, _____

h. disappear, go from sight, _____

i. grading, judging, _____

j. property, mansion, _____

k. tragedy, misfortune, _____

l. quickness, hurry, _____

m. head pain, discomfort, _____

n. shovel, digging tool, _____

o. shower, wash, _____

p. worried, concerned, _____

q. lunch, bread, _____

r. seller, clerk, _____

s. find, place, _____

t. pain, hurt, _____

4

Spelling Words

spade salesperson pavement behave locate grateful
debate rating estate haste bathe ache headache calendar
vanish sandwich anxious champion establish disaster

VI. Context Clues. Solve the word mysteries by using spelling words.

a. The water is ready. I will _____ the baby.

b. I have been lifting weights. My arms _____.

c. The magician pulled a scarf out of my ear. Then he seemed to make the scarf _____ into thin air.

d. The students chose a science problem for discussion. They will _____ it next week.

e. My friend is a gold medal winner. She is a _____.

f. The damage caused by the flood was terrible. It was a _____.

g. The clerk will assist you with your purchase. He is a _____.

h. Do not hurry. Work done in _____ makes waste.

i. Upon her death, her property was claimed by many. The court settled the _____.

j. My dog was missing last week. I was worried and _____ until I found her.

k. I have to lie down. I have a splitting _____.

l. The car was stolen two days ago. We have not been able to _____ it yet.

m. We had to dig up the yard to start a garden. We used a _____.

n. I think my birthday is on a Thursday. Please check the _____.

o. You cannot vote in that district. You must first _____ residence.

p. Children, please do not throw your crayons! You must _____.

q. That stock is a good investment. It has a high _____.

VII. Which One? Write the correct spelling words.

a. great
grate $\Big\rangle$ ful

b. sand $\Big\langle$ witch
wich

c. pave $\Big\langle$ ment
meant

_____ _____ _____

VIII. Finding Words. The words in the spelling list appear in the beginning (A-H), middle (I-Q), or end (R-Z) of the **Glossary/SPELLEX®**. Write each word.

Beginning A-H		Middle I-Q	End R-Z
1. _____	8. _____	1. _____	1. _____
2. _____	9. _____	2. _____	2. _____
3. _____	10. _____		3. _____
4. _____	11. _____		4. _____
5. _____	12. _____		5. _____
6. _____	13. _____		
7. _____			

IX. Write Your Journal. Use each of the spelling words or **Other Word Forms** (p. 3) to write a page in your journal about the day of the big storm. Circle the spelling words and the other word forms you used.

X. Final Test. Write each spelling word.

Lesson 2

I. Check Test. Write each spelling word.

II. Spelling Words and Phrases

evil	an **evil** deed
equal	must be **equal**
decent	**decent** behavior
recent	a **recent** event
meter	had read the water **meter**
medium	small, **medium**, or large
senior	a **senior** in high school
scene	**scene** of the crime
complete	when I **complete** it
supreme	a **supreme** effort
serious	a **serious** problem
severe	that **severe** blizzard
cheap	at a **cheap** price
treaty	signed the **treaty**
lease	a yearly **lease**
eager	an **eager** beginning
uneasy	an **uneasy** feeling
gear	shifted into low **gear**
disappear	might suddenly **disappear**
reflection	saw my **reflection**

III. Find a Fit. Write each word in its correct shape.

a.
b.
c.
d.
e.
f.
g.
h.
i.
j.
k.
l.
m.
n.
o.
p.
q.
r.
s.
t.

Other Word Forms

evilly, evilness, equaled, equaling, equally, equality, decently, decency, recently, metered, metric, media, median, seniority, scenery, completed, completing, completely, completion, supremely, seriously, seriousness, severely, severity, cheaper, cheaply, treaties, leases, leasing, eagerly, eagerness, easy, uneasily, gears, geared, appear, disappeared, disappearance, reflect, reflected, reflecting, reflections

IV. Sort Your Vowels. Write each spelling word in the correct list. A word may be used more than once.

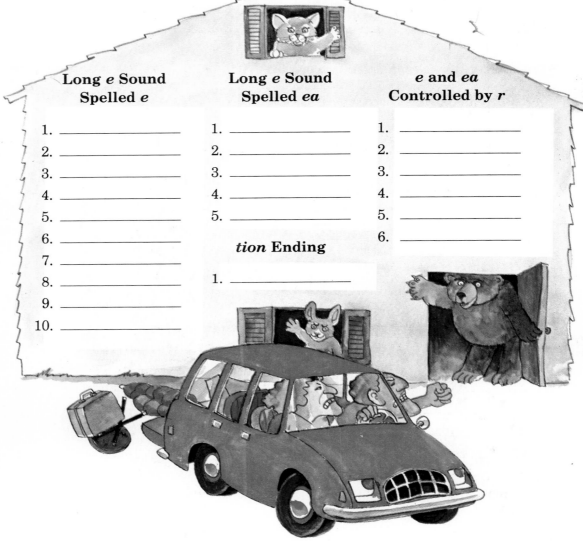

Long *e* Sound Spelled *e*

1. _____
2. _____
3. _____
4. _____
5. _____
6. _____
7. _____
8. _____
9. _____
10. _____

Long *e* Sound Spelled *ea*

1. _____
2. _____
3. _____
4. _____
5. _____

***tion* Ending**

1. _____

e* and *ea* Controlled by *r

1. _____
2. _____
3. _____
4. _____
5. _____
6. _____

V. Change a Word. Rearrange the letters in each underlined word to find a word from the spelling list. Write the word.

a. We visited the <u>center</u> of government on a _____ field trip.

b. Does that _____ creature <u>live</u> in this cave?

c. In a <u>rage</u>, the campers gathered their _____ and drove off.

d. I bought the <u>peach</u> for a _____ price.

e. The artist was forced to _____ an <u>easel</u>.

f. Both nations were _____ to <u>agree</u> to a truce.

Spelling Words

*evil   equal   decent   recent   meter   medium   senior   scene
complete   supreme   serious   severe   cheap   treaty   lease
eager   uneasy   gear   disappear   reflection*

VI. Crossword Puzzle. Solve the puzzle by using all the words from the spelling list. Check your answers in the **Glossary/SPELLEX®**.

Across

2. to finish
3. the same
5. anxious to do something
7. elder
12. nervous; restless
13. highest; greatest
15. a unit of measure
16. wicked
17. a likeness or image
18. not long ago

Down

1. a view
2. inexpensive
4. to rent
6. equipment
7. thoughtful; grave
8. harsh
9. to vanish
10. a written agreement between nations
11. small, _____, large
14. good; proper

9

VII. Hide and Seek. The spelling words can be found in the word puzzle. The words appear across, down, and diagonally. Circle and write the words.

Across

1.
2.
3.
4.
5.
6.
7.
8.
9.
10.
11.

d	e	c	e	n	t	e	v	i	l	m
s	i	h	a	w	v	s	y	e	s	e
a	j	s	q	u	n	e	a	s	y	d
r	s	c	a	a	k	v	m	l	m	i
e	c	o	m	p	l	e	t	e	m	u
f	e	m	s	u	p	r	e	m	e	m
l	n	t	l	t	e	e	j	l	t	d
e	e	r	e	m	l	e	a	g	e	r
c	h	e	a	p	g	e	a	r	r	e
t	j	a	s	e	n	i	o	r	j	c
i	g	t	e	m	p	r	s	g	g	e
o	l	y	g	e	q	u	a	l	p	n
n	a	s	e	r	i	o	u	s	d	t

Down

1.
2.
3.
4.
5.
6.
7.
8.

Diagonally

1.

VIII. All in a Sentence. Use each of the spelling words in sentences about a science-fiction adventure. You may use **Other Word Forms** (p. 7). Circle the spelling words and the other word forms you used.

Example: *Finally our space mission was* ⟨*completed*⟩ .

IX. Final Test. Write each spelling word.

10

Lesson 3

I. Check Test. Write each spelling word.

II. Spelling Words and Phrases

vice	no bad habit or **vice**
tile	a loose **tile** in the floor
spite	in **spite** of the weather
mining	**mining** for gold
idle	don't like to be **idle**
diet	now on a **diet**
diamond	sparkled like a **diamond**
finally	**finally** packed
trial	giving it a **trial**
quietly	to talk **quietly**
reliable	a **reliable** friend
infant	fed the **infant**
instant	started at the same **instant**
distant	the **distant** mountain
linen	made with **linen**
sicken	to **sicken** with fear
nickel	not much for a **nickel**
pickle	a very crisp **pickle**
tickled	**tickled** my nose
sprinkle	a light **sprinkle** of rain

III. Find a Fit. Write each word in its correct shape.

a.

b.

c.

d.

e.

f.

g.

h.

i.

j.

k.

l.

m.

n.

o.

p.

q.

r.

s.

t.

Other Word Forms

vices, vicious, tiles, tiled, tiling, spited, spiting, spiteful, mine, miner, idled, idling, idly, dieted, dieting, dieter, diamonds, final, finals, trials, quiet, rely, infants, infancy, instantly, distantly, distance, linens, sick, sickens, sickening, sickly, nickels, pickles, pickled, pickling, tickle, tickling, ticklish, sprinkles, sprinkled, sprinkling

IV. Rhyming Words.

a. Write the words from the spelling list that rhyme with each of the words.

1. chicken _____   7. sickle _____
2. dining _____   _____
3. quiet _____   8. crinkle _____
4. dial _____   9. quite _____
   _____   10. bridal _____
5. undeniable _____   11. trickled _____
6. spice _____

b. Write the three words not used above that rhyme with each other.

1. _____   2. _____   3. _____

c. Write the four words that did not rhyme with any of the words above.

1. _____   3. _____
2. _____   4. _____

V. Missing Vowels. Find the missing vowels and write the spelling words.

a. m __ n __ ng _____   g. d __ __ m __ nd _____
b. __ nf __ nt _____   h. q __ __ __ tly _____
c. l __ n __ n _____   i. d __ st __ nt _____
d. p __ ckl __ _____   j. t __ ckl __ d _____
e. spr __ nkl __ _____   k. r __ l __ __ bl __ _____
f. f __ n __ lly _____   l. s __ ck __ n _____

VI. Word Detective. Remove one letter from each underlined word to find a word from the spelling list. Write the word.

a. The audience loved them in _____ of their poor performance.   <u>sprite</u>

b. A bad habit can be a _____ .   <u>voice</u>

c. The feather _____ my nose.   <u>trickled</u>

d. A _____ is made from a cucumber.   <u>prickle</u>

e. Coal miners fear _____ accidents.   <u>minting</u>

f. Fine _____ is manufactured from flax.   <u>linden</u>

Spelling Words

*vice   tile   spite   mining   idle   diet   diamond   finally
trial   quietly   reliable   infant   instant   distant   linen
sicken   nickel   pickle   tickled   sprinkle*

VII. Finding Words. The words in the spelling list appear in the beginning (A-H), middle (I-Q), or end (R-Z) of the **Glossary/SPELLEX®**. Write each word.

Beginning A-H	Middle I-Q	End R-Z
1. _____	1. _____	1. _____
2. _____	2. _____	2. _____
3. _____	3. _____	3. _____
4. _____	4. _____	4. _____
	5. _____	5. _____
	6. _____	6. _____
	7. _____	7. _____
	8. _____	8. _____

VIII. Generally Speaking. Write a spelling word in the group it best fits.

a. steady, dependable, _____

b. penny, dime, _____

c. shower, water, _____

d. baby, child, _____

e. far, not close, _____

f. moment, second, _____

g. precious stone, gem, _____

h. silently, softly, _____

i. at last, at an end, _____

j. upset, make ill, _____

k. thin square, plastic piece, _____

IX. Change a Word. Rearrange the letters in each underlined word to find a word from the spelling list. Write the word.

    a. They <u>lied</u> when they said they were never _____ .

    b. It was a _____ for the hikers to remain so long on the <u>trail</u>.

    c. Every <u>tide</u> brings the large fish a new _____ of smaller fish.

X. Writing Sentences. Write each set of words in a sentence. You may use **Other Word Forms** (p. 11).

    1. infant—finally—quietly

    2. vice—spite—idle

    3. mining—distant—diamond

    4. sicken—diet—pickle

    5. tile—sprinkle—instant

    6. reliable—trial—nickel

    7. linen—tickled

XI. Final Test. Write each spelling word.

Lesson 4

I. Check Test. Write each spelling word.

II. Spelling Words and Phrases

sole	on the **sole** of my shoe
throne	was placed on the **throne**
postage	forgot the **postage** stamp
postpone	can't **postpone** the meeting
cooperate	asked them to **cooperate**
ghost	never saw a **ghost**
stroll	liked to **stroll** together
thrown	will be **thrown** out
organize	to **organize** a second team
force	the **force** of the water
perform	loves to **perform**
reform	must **reform** behavior
resort	a summer **resort**
import	went to the **import** store
explore	want to **explore** the cave
enforce	a way to **enforce** the law
according	**according** to our records
broad	a **broad** avenue
abroad	a trip **abroad** to Greece
coarse	**coarse** texture of cloth

III. Find a Fit. Write each word in its correct shape.

a.
b.
c.
d.
e.
f.
g.
h.
i.
j.
k.
l.
m.
n.
o.
p.
q.
r.
s.
t.

Other Word Forms

soles, soled, thrones, post, postal, postponed, postponing, postponement, cooperated, cooperation, ghostly, strolled, stroller, throw, threw, organized, organization, organizer, forced, forcibly, performed, performer, performance, reformed, reformer, resorts, resorted, imports, importer, explores, explored, exploring, explorer, exploration, enforced, enforcer, accord, broader, broadly, coarser, coarsest, coarsely

15

IV. Hide and Seek.
The spelling words and some **Other Word Forms** (p. 15) can be found in the grid below. The words appear across and down. Circle and write the words.

Spelling Words

Across

1. ⬜⬜⬜⬜⬜
2. ⬜⬜⬜⬜⬜
3. ⬜⬜⬜⬜⬜⬜⬜
4. ⬜⬜⬜⬜⬜
5. ⬜⬜⬜⬜
6. ⬜⬜⬜⬜
7. ⬜⬜⬜⬜⬜⬜
8. ⬜⬜⬜⬜⬜
9. ⬜⬜⬜⬜
10. ⬜⬜⬜⬜⬜⬜
11. ⬜⬜⬜⬜⬜
12. ⬜⬜⬜⬜⬜⬜⬜

Down

1. ⬜⬜⬜⬜⬜⬜
2. ⬜⬜⬜⬜⬜
3. ⬜⬜⬜⬜⬜⬜⬜
4. ⬜⬜⬜
5. ⬜⬜⬜⬜⬜⬜
6. ⬜⬜⬜⬜⬜⬜
7. ⬜⬜⬜⬜⬜
8. ⬜⬜⬜⬜⬜⬜

```
r e f o r m i s n i r o a e
e f o r c e d o e e e d b x
s t h r o w n l g n x s r p
o r g a n i z e b f p c o l
r p f c s o l e s o l o a o
t h r o n e e o b r o a d r
t t s o g h o s t c r r p i
i s l p c o a r s e e s e n
m w a e s t r o l l l e r g
p f o r c e i w t i l r f t
o a l a p o s t p o n e o h
r n l t s t r o l l e d r r
t e r e i p o s t a g e m e
d a c c o r d i n g j p i w
```

Other Word Forms

Across

1. ⬜⬜⬜⬜⬜⬜
2. ⬜⬜⬜⬜
3. ⬜⬜⬜⬜⬜⬜

Down

1. ⬜⬜⬜⬜⬜⬜⬜⬜
2. ⬜⬜⬜⬜⬜⬜
3. ⬜⬜⬜⬜

V. Finding Words.
The words in the spelling list appear in the beginning (A-H), middle (I-Q), or end (R-Z) of the **Glossary/SPELLEX®**. Write each word.

Beginning A-H		Middle I-Q	End R-Z
1. _____	6. _____	1. _____	1. _____
2. _____	7. _____	2. _____	2. _____
3. _____	8. _____	3. _____	3. _____
4. _____	9. _____	4. _____	4. _____
5. _____		5. _____	5. _____
			6. _____

Spelling Words

sole   throne   postage   postpone   cooperate   ghost   stroll
thrown   organize   force   perform   reform   resort   import
explore   enforce   according   broad   abroad   coarse

VI. Scrambled Words. Unscramble the scrambled word to find the spelling word that completes the sentence. Write the word.

Scrambled Words

a. The actors will _____ every evening for two weeks.   rmofrep

b. I enjoy a leisurely _____ through the park.   lolstr

c. How much _____ did the letter require?   stopeag

d. We _____ cheese from other countries.   oprtim

e. _____ to my records, the bill was never paid.   ngrdaiocc

f. Adventurers _____ faraway lands.   pleexor

g. If we _____, we will succeed in solving the problem.   rooteeapc

h. The vacation _____ is in Florida.   rtsero

i. The clown always wears a _____ smile.   daobr

j. The _____ of the river carried me into deep water.   coref

k. We sailed _____ on the ocean liner.   adaobr

l. Blackbeard's _____ still haunts the island.   stogh

m. The mayoral candidate is calling for a tax _____.   ferorm

n. We must _____ the meeting until Saturday.   stoneopp

o. The new secretary was hired to _____ the files.   neogairz

p. Police officers _____ the laws.   rceeonf

Homophones. Write the word from the spelling list that is a homophone for each word.

    a. thrown   ———————————

    b. soul   ———————————

    c. course   ———————————

    d. throne   ———————————

VIII. **Writing Sentences.** Write each set of words in a sentence. You may use **Other Word Forms** (p. 15).

1. postpone—perform—resort

2. postage—thrown—stroll

3. according—sole—explore

4. ghost—organize—force

5. reform—enforce—broad

6. throne—abroad—import

7. coarse—cooperate

MT. KATAHDIN
AMC LODGE

IX. Final Test. Write each spelling word.

Lesson 5

I. Check Test. Write each spelling word.

II. Spelling Words and Phrases

refuse	didn't dare to **refuse**
confuse	doesn't **confuse** me
dispute	a **dispute** about the goal
amusement	into the **amusement** park
useless	because it's **useless**
issue	the new magazine **issue**
statue	stood like a **statue**
value	of little **value**
valuable	a **valuable** painting
discontinue	will **discontinue** the model
union	joined the labor **union**
human	the strongest **human** alive
humor	the book of **humor**
jury	met with the **jury**
curious	a **curious** cat
figure	if you can **figure** out
future	sometime in the **future**
injure	might **injure** your hand
insure	will **insure** the package
capture	will **capture** the flag

III. Find a Fit. Write each word in its correct shape.

a.
b.
c.
d.
e.
f.
g.
h.
i.
j.
k.
l.
m.
n.
o.
p.
q.
r.
s.
t.

Other Word Forms

refused, refusing, refusal, confusing, confusion, disputed, disputing, amuse, amusing, amusements, use, uselessly, uselessness, issues, issued, issuing, statues, statuette, value, valued, valuing, continue, discontinued, unionized, unions, humanity, humanly, humorous, humorist, juries, curiosity, curiousness, figured, figurine, futuristic, injuring, injurious, insuring, insurance, captured, capturing

IV. All in a Row. Write the twenty spelling words in alphabetical order. Then join the boxed letters and write four hidden words.

1. — — — — — — — — ☐

2. — — — — — ☐ — —

3. — ☐ — — — — —

4. — — — — ☐ — —

5. — — — — ☐ — — — —

Hidden Word: _____

6. — — — — — ☐ —

7. — — — — ☐ —

8. — — — — ☐

9. — — ☐ —

10. — — — ☐☐

Hidden Word: _____

11. ☐ — — — — —

12. — ☐ — — — —

13. — ☐ — ☐ — —

14. — — ☐ —

15. — — — — — ☐

Hidden Word: _____

16. — — — ☐ — —

17. — ☐ — ☐ —

18. — ☐ — — — — — —

19. — — — — — — ☐

20. — — ☐ — — —

Hidden Word: _____

V. Fan Out. Write the spelling word formed by each combination.

1. _____
2. _____
3. _____
4. _____
5. _____

fig
fut
inj
ins
capt

ure

Spelling Words

refuse confuse dispute amusement useless issue statue
value valuable discontinue union human humor
jury curious figure future injure insure capture

VI. Bases, Prefixes, and Suffixes. The spelling list contains sixteen base words and four words with prefixes or suffixes. Write each spelling word.

Words With Prefixes or Suffixes	Base Words	Words With Prefixes or Suffixes	Base Words
a. figurine	_____	k. captured	_____
b. confusion	_____	l. disputed	_____
c. humorous	_____	m. valuing	_____
d. curiosity	_____	n. futuristic	_____
e. injurious	_____	o. unionized	_____
f. refusal	_____	p. juries	_____
g. issues	_____	q. _____	use
h. insurance	_____	r. _____	value
i. humanity	_____	s. _____	amuse
j. statuette	_____	t. _____	continue

VII. Look-alikes. Some words have the same spelling but different meanings and different pronunciations. These words are called *homographs*. Use the **Glossary/SPELLEX®** to check the meanings of the homographs below. Then use each homograph in a sentence.

    a. re fuse'

    b. ref' use

VIII. Building Sentences. Write the following phrases in sentences.

    a. sense of <u>humor</u>

    b. their <u>amusement</u>

    c. <u>useless</u> machine

    d. silly <u>dispute</u>

    e. on the <u>statue</u>

    f. <u>valuable</u> stamp

    g. <u>curious</u> children

    h. shadowy <u>figure</u>

    i. confused the <u>jury</u>

    j. <u>future</u> plans

    k. will need to <u>insure</u>

    l. may <u>injure</u> my back

    m. current <u>issue</u>

    n. to <u>capture</u> the flag

    o. <u>union</u> meeting

    p. <u>human</u> nature

    q. will <u>discontinue</u> the magazine

    r. to <u>confuse</u> the class

    s. may <u>refuse</u> to go

    t. of little <u>value</u>

IX. Final Test. Write each spelling word.

1	2	3	4	5
idle	anxious	establish	statue	salesperson
infant	eager	resort	recent	cheap
ghost	instant	mining	spade	refuse
haste	throne	organize	enforce	complete
evil	diamond	issue	curious	human

I. Word Operations. Unscramble each scrambled word to form a spelling word. The number tells you in what column you can find the spelling word. Write the word. Then perform one or two operations on each word to write other word forms.

	Spelling Words	**Operations**	**Other Word Forms**
a. lide = (1)	_____	+ ness =	_____
b. blishatse = (3)	_____	+ ment =	_____
c. manhu = (5)	_____	+ ity =	_____
d. ragee = (2)	_____	+ ly =	_____
e. live = (1)	_____	+ s =	_____
f. nagorize = (3)	_____	− e + ing =	_____
g. chape = (5)	_____	+ ly =	_____
h. daesp = (4)	_____	+ s =	_____
i. center = (4)	_____	+ ly =	_____
j. onethr = (2)	_____	+ s =	_____
k. forence = (4)	_____	+ ment =	_____
l. fuseer = (5)	_____	+ s =	_____
m. hesta = (1)	_____	− e + ens =	_____
n. sorter = (3)	_____	+ ing =	_____
o. siouxan = (2)	_____	+ ly =	_____
p. ingmin = (3)	_____	− ing + ers =	_____
q. pleetmoc = (5)	_____	+ ly =	_____
r. rucsiou = (4)	_____	− us + sity =	_____
s. stogh = (1)	_____	+ ly =	_____
t. stantin = (2)	_____	+ ly =	_____
u. sueis = (3)	_____	− e + ing =	_____
v. stueta = (4)	_____	+ s =	_____
w. mondaid = (2)	_____	+ s =	_____
x. fantin = (1)	_____	− t + cy =	_____

Write the plural form of *salesperson.* _____

6

1	2	3	4	5
calendar	tile	debate	according	equal
tickled	dispute	spite	jury	disaster
insure	rating	future	distant	trial
decent	abroad	lease	reform	treaty
medium	broad	grateful	import	union

II. Words in Blanks. Write other word forms or the spelling words to complete the sentences. The number tells you in what column you can find the spelling word. Write each word or its other word form only once. If you need help, use the **Glossary/SPELLEX®**.

a. The kitchen (2) _____ were cut (5) _____ on all sides.

b. No one (2) _____ the fact that (1) _____ are helpful.

c. The (2) _____ for the new television shows are low,

(4) _____ to the newscaster.

d. Lawyers have always (3) _____ the ways (4) _____ are selected.

e. Heavy smoke in the (4) _____ signaled a (5) _____ fire.

f. In (3) _____ of my collar, the feathers on my hat kept

(1) _____ my neck.

g. The lawyers traveled (2) _____ to study court (5) _____ in Europe.

h. Saving money may (1) _____ a good (3) _____ .

i. By (4) _____ your study habits, you can get (1) _____ marks on your report card.

j. One company (4) _____ typewriters and (3) _____ them to offices.

k. Though we are both of (1) _____ height, my shoulders are

(2) _____ than yours.

l. Peace (5) _____ are often (3) _____ accepted by warring nations.

m. There are many labor (5) _____ in our country.

1	2	3	4	5	**6**
sandwich	behave	bathe	headache	ache	
senior	disappear	reflection	scene	meter	
diet	nickel	sprinkle	pickle	quietly	
thrown	stroll	explore	postage	cooperate	
injure	amusement	capture	valuable	discontinue	

III. Calendar of Events. Use other word forms or the spelling words to write a silly or serious note on each day of the school calendar. Circle the other word forms and the spelling words you used. Two days are filled out for you.

MON	TUES	WED	THURS	FRI
1	2 *We (explored) the woods.*	3	4	5
8	9	10	11	12
15	16	17	18 *ate ten (pickles)*	19
22	23	24	25	26

6

1	2	3	4	5
gear	locate	pavement	vanish	estate
supreme	figure	serious	confuse	value
sicken	linen	reliable	finally	vice
postpone	perform	force	coarse	sole
uneasy	humor	champion	severe	useless

IV. Sentence Completion. Use other word forms or the spelling words to replace the words printed under the blanks. If you need help, use the **Glossary/SPELLEX®**.

a. We _____ the play today because it was _____ yesterday.
   (perform)   (postpone)

b. I _____ on the cobbler to mend the _____ of my shoes.
   (reliable)   (sole)

c. Our newly _____ driveway has a much _____ surface
   (pavement)   (coarse)
   than most.

d. Each New Year, some people try _____ to give up their bad habits,
   (serious)
   or _____ .
   (vice)

e. We _____ all ten _____ on our bicycles to pedal uphill.
   (useless)   (gear)

f. Some people are _____ telling _____ stories.
   (uneasy)   (humor)

g. Three private _____ are _____ near the ocean.
   (estate)   (locate)

h. Though I felt _____ to my stomach before class, I _____
   (sicken)   (force)
   myself to redo my math _____ .
   (figure)

i. My _____ stamp collection was damaged _____ during
   (value)   (severe)
   the flood.

j. When I couldn't find the bed _____ , I was sure they had
   (linen)

   _____ .
   (vanish)

k. The tennis match for the _____ was played _____ .
   (champion)   (supreme)

l. I became _____ during the _____ exam in math class.
   (confuse)   (finally)

Lesson 7

I. Check Test. Write each spelling word.

II. Spelling Words and Phrases

raid	a **raid** at night
vain	tried in **vain**
raisin	**raisin** and nut bread
claims	**claims** the prize
exclaim	will **exclaim** angrily
contain	a box to **contain** supplies
attain	will **attain** our goals
obtain	will **obtain** another one
entertain	likes to **entertain**
explain	no need to **explain**
chamber	a secret **chamber**
mass	a swarming **mass** of hornets
rascal	called me a **rascal**
staff	met with the **staff**
standard	a **standard** size
exact	the **exact** change
unpack	had to **unpack** in the dark
margin	the **margin** on the left
bargain	made a **bargain**
uncertain	**uncertain** future

III. Find a Fit. Write each word in its correct shape.

a. ☐☐☐☐

b. ☐☐☐☐

c. ☐☐☐☐☐

d. ☐☐☐☐☐☐

e. ☐☐☐☐☐☐

f. ☐☐☐☐☐

g. ☐☐☐☐☐☐☐☐

h. ☐☐☐☐☐☐☐

i. ☐☐☐☐☐☐

j. ☐☐☐☐☐☐

k. ☐☐☐☐☐☐

l. ☐☐☐☐☐☐☐

m. ☐☐☐☐☐☐

n. ☐☐☐☐☐

o. ☐☐☐☐☐☐☐☐☐

p. ☐☐☐☐☐☐

q. ☐☐☐☐☐

r. ☐☐☐☐☐☐☐

s. ☐☐☐☐☐☐

t. ☐☐☐☐☐☐

Other Word Forms

raided, raider, vainly, vanity, raisins, claim, claiming, exclaimed, exclamation, containing, container, attains, attained, obtaining, obtainable, entertainer, entertainment, explained, explaining, explanation, chambers, masses, massed, rascals, staffed, staffing, standards, exactness, exactly, pack, unpacked, unpacking, marginal, bargained, bargainer, certain, uncertainty

IV. Synonym Puzzles. Find a synonym from the spelling list to complete each puzzle. Write each word. Use the **Glossary/SPELLEX®**.

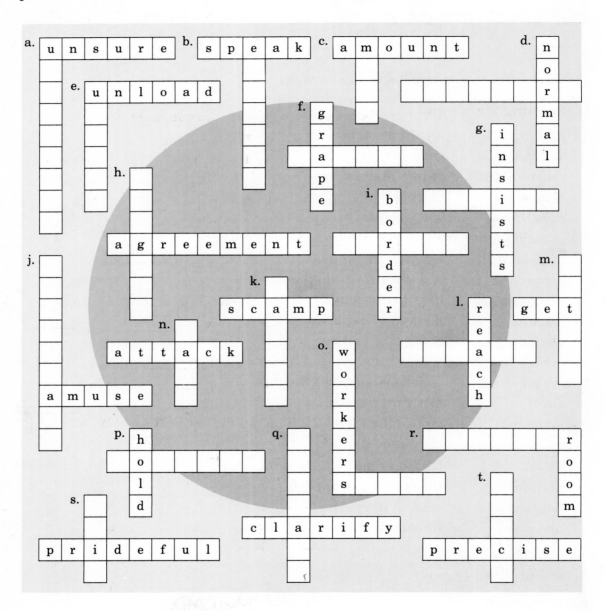

a. u n s u r e

b. s p e a k

c. a m o u n t

d. n o r m a l

e. u n l o a d

f. g r a p e

g. i n s i s t s

h. a g r e e m e n t

i. b o r d e r

j.

k. s c a m p

l. r e a c h / r _ g e t

m.

n. a t t a c k

o. w o r k e r s

p. h o l d

q. c l a r i f y

r. r o o m

s. p r i d e f u l

t. p r e c i s e

a m u s e

Spelling Words

raid vain raisin claims exclaim contain attain obtain entertain explain chamber mass rascal staff standard exact unpack margin bargain uncertain

V. Bases, Prefixes, and Suffixes. The spelling list contains seventeen base words and three words with prefixes or suffixes. Write each spelling word.

Words With Prefixes or Suffixes	Base Words	Words With Prefixes or Suffixes	Base Words
a. raisins	_____	k. raider	_____
b. attained	_____	l. vainly	_____
c. masses	_____	m. staffed	_____
d. container	_____	n. entertainment	_____
e. rascals	_____	o. chambers	_____
f. exclaimed	_____	p. explaining	_____
g. standards	_____	q. exactly	_____
h. obtaining	_____	r. _____	certain
i. bargained	_____	s. _____	pack
j. marginal	_____	t. _____	claim

VI. Finding Words. The words in the spelling list appear in the beginning (A-H), middle (I-Q), or end (R-Z) of the **Glossary/SPELLEX®**. Write each word.

Beginning A-H		Middle I-Q	End R-Z
1. _____	6. _____	1. _____	1. _____
2. _____	7. _____	2. _____	2. _____
3. _____	8. _____	3. _____	3. _____
4. _____	9. _____		4. _____
5. _____			5. _____
			6. _____
			7. _____
			8. _____

VII. Rewriting as Questions. Rewrite these sentences as questions.

    a. They will <u>entertain</u> the others.   *Will they entertain the others?*

    b. She will <u>unpack</u> the <u>raisin</u> box last.

    c. We did hear them <u>exclaim</u> with joy.

    d. You must leave a <u>margin</u> on your paper.

    e. The <u>standard</u> for the parts is <u>exact</u>.

    f. He will <u>obtain</u> a permit.

    g. The little <u>rascal</u> was quite <u>vain</u>.

    h. You were <u>uncertain</u> about the <u>claims</u>.

    i. The <u>staff</u> had planned the <u>raid</u>.

    j. They did know what the <u>chamber</u> would <u>contain</u>.

    k. You will <u>explain</u> why we made the <u>bargain</u>.

    l. It was a sticky <u>mass</u>.

    m. We will <u>attain</u> our goal.

VIII. Final Test. Write each spelling word.

Lesson 8

I. Check Test. Write each spelling word.

II. Spelling Words and Phrases

creep	will **creep** away
speech	forgot the **speech**
squeeze	can't **squeeze** through
weekly	**weekly** newspaper
needless	**needless** to say
proceed	would **proceed** cautiously
agreement	signed the **agreement**
peer	to **peer** into the dark
steer	will **steer** with both hands
brief	a very **brief** stay
grief	hid our **grief**
thief	caught the **thief**
niece	a **niece** and a nephew
pier	at the end of the **pier**
neither	**neither** here nor there
received	**received** in the mail
energy	will save **energy**
machinery	modern **machinery**
convince	will **convince** the jury
medicine	rarely needs **medicine**

III. Find a Fit. Write each word in its correct shape.

a.
b.
c.
d.
e.
f.
g.
h.
i.
j.
k.
l.
m.
n.
o.
p.
q.
r.
s.
t.

Other Word Forms

crept, creeping, creepy, speeches, squeezes, squeezed, squeezing, week, need, needlessly, proceeds, proceeded, procedure, agree, agreements, peers, peering, steers, steered, steering, briefly, briefer, grieve, grieves, grieving, thieves, theft, nieces, piers, receive, receiving, energies, energize, machine, convinces, convinced, convincing, medicines, medicinal

IV. Generally Speaking. Write each spelling word in the group it best fits.

a. wharf, dock, _____

b. prescription, treatment, _____

c. grip, grab, _____

d. contract, understanding, _____

e. persuade, win over, _____

f. equipment, tools, _____

g. go on, continue, _____

h. fuel, power, _____

i. unnecessary, unimportant, _____

j. got, accepted, _____

k. daily, monthly, _____

l. none, not any, _____

m. crawl, slide, _____

n. cousin, nephew, _____

o. talk, announcement, _____

p. criminal, burglar, _____

q. look, gaze, _____

r. short, quick, _____

s. guide, direct, _____

t. sadness, sorrow, _____

Spelling Words

creep speech squeeze weekly needless proceed agreement peer steer brief grief thief niece pier neither received energy machinery convince medicine

V. Break the Code. Use the code to write the spelling words.

a	b	c	d	e	f	g	h	i	j	k	l	m	n	o	p	q	r	s	t	u	v	w	x	y	z
↓	↓	↓	↓	↓	↓	↓	↓	↓	↓	↓	↓	↓	↓	↓	↓	↓	↓	↓	↓	↓	↓	↓	↓	↓	↓
q	e	o	j	v	s	a	g	p	y	i	x	b	r	c	h	t	d	m	z	w	k	l	f	n	u

a. qpkbx _____

b. fqbbn _____

c. sbrkokyb _____

d. ocyekyob _____

e. ybkqpbn _____

f. ybbrwbff _____

g. mnkbx _____

h. incobbr _____

i. ubbvwj _____

j. onbbi _____

k. ikbn _____

l. hnkbx _____

m. fibbop _____

n. fazbbtb _____

o. ibbn _____

p. bybnhj _____

q. ykbob _____

r. sgopkybnj _____

s. nbobkebr _____

t. ghnbbsbyq _____

VI. Sort Your *E* Sounds. Find the missing vowels and write the spelling words.

a. gr __ __ f _____

b. sp __ __ ch _____

c. n __ __ ther _____

d. st __ __ r _____

e. p __ __ r _____

f. p __ __ r _____

g. w __ __ kly _____

h. br __ __ f _____

i. cr __ __ p _____

j. th __ __ f _____

k. proc __ __ d _____

l. rec __ __ ved _____

m. n __ __ dless _____

n. n __ __ ce _____

o. squ __ __ ze _____

p. agr __ __ ment _____

33

VII. Bases and Suffixes. The spelling list contains fifteen base words and five words with suffixes. Write each spelling word.

Words With Suffixes	Base Words	Words With Suffixes	Base Words
a. steering	_____	k. medicines	_____
b. piers	_____	l. briefly	_____
c. speeches	_____	m. convinces	_____
d. energies	_____	n. grieves	_____
e. squeezed	_____	o. _____ week	
f. nieces	_____	p. _____ receive	
g. proceeded	_____	q. _____ need	
h. peering	_____	r. _____ machine	
i. thieves	_____	s. _____ agree	
j. creeping	_____		

Write the one base word not used above. _____

VIII. All in a Sentence. Use each of the spelling words in a sentence about one of the following titles. You may use **Other Word Forms** (p. 31). Circle the spelling words and the other word forms you used.

Return From an Ocean Adventure or Forgive and Forget

Example: *The cautious animal* (crept) *from the* (pier).

IX. Final Test. Write each spelling word.

Lesson 9

I. Check Test. Write each spelling word.

II. Spelling Words and Phrases

minor	**minor** or major
silent	**silent** approval
private	**private** property
primary	**primary** colors
horizon	beyond the **horizon**
advice	good bit of **advice**
polite	a **polite** greeting
dislike	a strong **dislike**
decline	will **decline** the offer
inclined	**inclined** to agree
unwise	**unwise** decision
arrive	will **arrive** at five
excitement	concealed their **excitement**
admire	had to **admire**
desire	to **desire** a new desk
inquire	will **inquire** within
umpire	the jumpy **umpire**
entirely	**entirely** alone
obey	tries to **obey**
greater	lesser or **greater**

III. Find a Fit. Write each word in its correct shape.

a.
b.
c.
d.
e.
f.
g.
h.
i.
j.
k.
l.
m.
n.
o.
p.
q.
r.
s.
t.

Other Word Forms

minors, minority, silently, silence, privately, privacy, prime, primaries, horizons, horizontal, advise, advising, adviser, politely, politeness, like, disliked, disliking, declined, declining, incline, inclining, wise, unwisely, arriving, arrival, excite, exciting, admiring, admirable, desiring, desirable, inquiring, inquiry, umpired, umpires, entire, entirety, obeyed, obeying, great, greatly

IV. Sort Your Vowels.

a. In alphabetical order, write the spelling words that have the vowel sound of long *i* in the first syllable.

1. _____   3. _____

2. _____   4. _____

b. In alphabetical order, write the spelling words that have the vowel sound of long *i* in the second syllable. Include words in which *r* follows long *i*.

1. _____   6. _____   11. _____

2. _____   7. _____   12. _____

3. _____   8. _____   13. _____

4. _____   9. _____   14. _____

5. _____   10. _____

c. Two spelling words do not have the vowel sound of long *i*. They are

_____ and _____ .

36

Spelling Words

minor silent private primary horizon advice polite
dislike decline inclined unwise arrive excitement admire
desire inquire umpire entirely obey greater

V. Words and Meanings. Write a spelling word for each meaning. Then read down each column to find three more spelling words.

a. a person who rules in sports ___ [ ] ___ ___ ___ ___

b. a suggestion about doing something ___ ___ ___ [ ] ___ ___

c. completely ___ [ ] ___ ___ ___ ___ ___ ___

d. showing good manners ___ [ ] ___ ___ ___ ___

e. to look at with wonder ___ ___ ___ ___ [ ] ___ ___

f. foolish ___ ___ ___ ___ [ ] ___

g. to appear ___ ___ ___ ___ [ ] ___ ___

h. willing or tending ___ ___ ___ [ ] ___ ___ ___

i. not for public use ___ ___ ___ ___ ___ [ ] ___

j. to ask about something ___ [ ] ___ ___ ___ ___ ___

k. larger ___ ___ ___ ___ [ ] ___ ___

l. to refuse politely [ ] ___ ___ ___ ___ ___ ___

m. to do what one is told ___ ___ [ ] ___ ___

n. to care little for ___ ___ [ ] ___ ___ ___ ___

o. a line where earth and sky seem to meet ___ ___ ___ [ ] ___ ___ ___ ___

p. first in importance ___ [ ] ___ ___ ___ ___ ___

q. enthusiasm ___ ___ ___ ___ [ ] ___ ___ ___ ___

Write the spelling words made by each set of boxes.

_____   _____   _____

VI. Hidden Words.
Hidden Words. The spelling words can be found in the word puzzle. The words appear across and down. Circle and write the words.

Across

1.
2.
3.
4.
5.
6.
7.
8.
9.
10.
11.
12.

Down

1.
2.
3.
4.
5.
6.
7.
8.

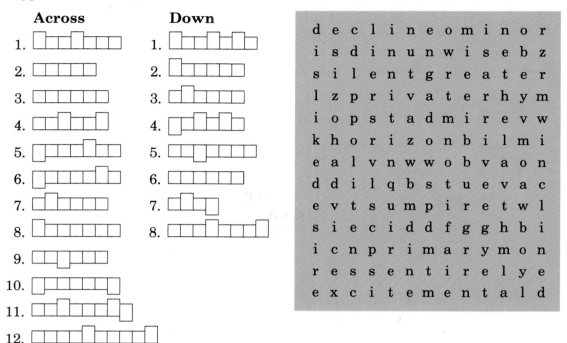

```
d e c l i n e o m i n o r
i s d i n u n w i s e b z
s i l e n t g r e a t e r
l z p r i v a t e r h y m
i o p s t a d m i r e v w
k h o r i z o n b i l m i
e a l v n w w o b v a o n
d d i l q b s t u e v a c
e v t s u m p i r e t w l
s i e c i d d f g g h b i
i c n p r i m a r y m o n
r e s s e n t i r e l y e
e x c i t e m e n t a l d
```

VII. Writing Headlines.
Writing Headlines. Use all the spelling words to write headlines. You may use **Other Word Forms** (p. 35). Circle the spelling words and the other word forms you used.

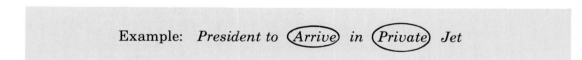

Example: *President to* (*Arrive*) *in* (*Private*) *Jet*

VIII. Final Test.
Final Test. Write each spelling word.

Lesson 10

I. Check Test. Write each spelling word.

II. Spelling Words and Phrases

poultry	**poultry** farm
shoulder	injured my **shoulder**
source	our only **source**
journey	at the end of the **journey**
tournament	a soccer **tournament**
total	**total** defeat
noble	a **noble** gesture
notice	without **notice**
motion	an unsteady **motion**
groceries	bought the **groceries**
nowhere	**nowhere** but here
photograph	a family **photograph**
overflow	will **overflow** into the sewer
glory	shared the **glory**
porter	signaled the **porter**
normal	a **normal** temperature
foreign	a **foreign** country
important	not very **important**
continent	the **continent** of Africa
contribute	will **contribute** to charity

III. Find a Fit. Write each word in its correct shape.

a.
b.
c.
d.
e.
f.
g.
h.
i.
j.
k.
l.
m.
n.
o.
p.
q.
r.
s.
t.

Other Word Forms

shouldered, shouldering, sources, journeyed, tournaments, totaled, totaling, totally, totality, nobler, noblest, nobly, notices, noticed, notable, noticing, motions, motioned, motioning, grocery, photographs, photography, photographer, overflowed, overflowing, glories, glorify, glorious, porters, normally, normality, foreigner, importance, continents, contributions

IV. Sort Your O's. In alphabetical order, write the spelling words in the correct boxes.

Words With r-controlled o

1. _____
2. _____
3. _____
4. _____
5. _____

Words With ou

1. _____
2. _____
3. _____
4. _____
5. _____

Words With Long o

1. _____   5. _____
2. _____   6. _____
3. _____   7. _____
4. _____   8. _____

Write the two words that did not fit in any box.

1. _____
2. _____

V. Generally Speaking. Write each spelling word in the group it best fits.

a. wrist, elbow, _____

b. observe, see, _____

c. flood, spill, _____

d. strange, alien, _____

e. foods, supplies, _____

f. travel, voyage, _____

g. usual, regular, _____

h. fame, honor, _____

i. birds, chickens, _____

j. give, offer, _____

k. competition, contests, _____

l. land mass, country, _____

m. movement, action, _____

n. complete, entire, _____

o. start, beginning, _____

p. carrier, attendant, _____

q. generous, grand, _____

r. picture, snapshot, _____

s. serious, valuable, _____

t. no place, not anywhere, _____

40

Spelling Words

*poultry   shoulder   source   journey   tournament   total   noble
notice   motion   groceries   nowhere   photograph   overflow   glory
porter   normal   foreign   important   continent   contribute*

VI. Crossword Puzzle. Solve the puzzle by using all the words from the spelling list. Check your answers in the **Glossary/SPELLEX®**.

Across

2. a long trip
5. food items
8. a person who carries luggage
9. to spill over
11. not silly
16. the beginning
17. the full amount
18. a person of high rank
19. not anywhere
20. the largest piece of land

Down

1. a picture
3. usual
4. honor
6. a part of the body
7. to give
10. from another country
12. ducks, geese, and chickens
13. a series of contests
14. an important message
15. movement

VII. Who Am I? Solve the puzzle and read down the column to discover two characters from a classic children's story. All the words can be found in the spelling list. One word will be an **Other Word Form** (p. 39).*

a. chickens ___ ___ ___ ___ ___ ☐ ___

b. where a river begins ___ ☐ ___ ___ ___ ___

c. person of high rank ___ ___ ☐ ___ ___ ___

d. movement ___ ___ ___ ☐ ___ ___

e. not anywhere ☐ ___ ___ ___ ___ ___

f. snapshot ___ ☐ ___ ___ ___ ___ ___

g. food supplies ___ ___ ☐ ___ ___ ___ ___

h. spill over ___ ___ ___ ___ ___ ___ ☐ ___

i. upper arm ___ ___ ___ ___ ___ ___ ☐ ___ ___

j. usual ___ ___ ___ ___ ☐ ___

k. large land mass ___ ___ ___ ___ ___ ___ ___ ☐ ___

l. observed* ___ ___ ___ ___ ___ ☐

m. a series of contests ___ ___ ___ ___ ___ ___ ☐ ___ ___ ___

n. the sum ___ ___ ___ ☐ ___

o. fame or honor ___ ___ ___ ☐ ___

p. from another country ___ ___ ___ ___ ☐ ___ ___

q. necessary ___ ___ ___ ___ ___ ☐ ___ ___

r. a trip ___ ___ ___ ___ ☐ ___ ___

The two characters are _____ .

VIII. Final Test. Write each spelling word.

42

Lesson 11

I. Check Test. Write each spelling word.

II. Spelling Words and Phrases

adventure	new **adventure** books
natural	only **natural** food
funeral	**funeral** march
musical	**musical** chairs
manual	the teacher's **manual**
manufacturing	a **manufacturing** city
rude	**rude** and crude
include	does **include** tax
introduce	can **introduce** my friend
reduce	must **reduce** speed
produce	will **produce** a product
salute	to **salute** the flag
cruel	cold, **cruel** winds
truthful	always **truthful**
through	**through** the woods
proof	a **proof** of guilt
gloomy	**gloomy** day
jewels	stars like **jewels**
screwdriver	a hammer and **screwdriver**
tour	a four-week **tour**

III. Find a Fit. Write each word in its correct shape.

a.

b.

c.

d.

e.

f.

g.

h.

i.

j.

k.

l.

m.

n.

o.

p.

q.

r.

s.

t.

Other Word Forms

adventures, adventurous, nature, naturally, funerals, music, musician, manuals, manually, manufacture, manufactured, rudest, rudely, included, including, introduced, introducing, introduction, reduced, reducing, reduction, produced, producing, production, saluted, saluting, crueler, cruelly, cruelty, truth, truthfully, prove, proving, gloom, gloomiest, jewel, jewelry, screwdrivers, toured, tourist

IV. Sort Your _U_'s. Write each spelling word in the correct box. One word goes in more than one box.

Letter _u_ in the First or Only Syllable	
1. _____	5. _____
2. _____	6. _____
3. _____	7. _____
4. _____	

Letter _u_ in the Third Syllable
1. _____
2. _____

Letter _u_ in the Second Syllable	
1. _____	5. _____
2. _____	6. _____
3. _____	7. _____
4. _____	8. _____

Words Without the Letter _u_
1. _____
2. _____
3. _____
4. _____

V. Guide Words. These word pairs are guide words from the **Glossary/SPELLEX®.** Write the words from the spelling list that appear on the same page as each pair of guide words.

Example:

labor—machine
landlord
loyal

abandon—adventure
1. _____

concern—cushion
2. _____

favor—future
3. _____

gallop—height
4. _____

hesitate—insect
5. _____

insects—knowledge
6. _____
7. _____

machinery—mining
8. _____
9. _____

minor—nowhere
10. _____
11. _____

power—publish
12. _____
13. _____

punctual—refuse
14. _____

regard—scarce
15. _____
16. _____

scarcely—sicken
17. _____

theater—treat
18. _____
19. _____

treatment—various
20. _____

Spelling Words

adventure natural funeral musical manual manufacturing rude include introduce reduce produce salute cruel truthful through proof gloomy jewels screwdriver tour

VI. Careers. Using words from the spelling list, complete each statement about various careers.

a. Farmers would want their land to _____ healthy crops.

b. A police detective would insist on _____ .

c. A travel agent would plan a _____ .

d. A soldier would be expected to _____ .

e. A do-it-yourself repairer would read a _____ .

f. A composer might write a Broadway _____ .

g. A carpenter would require the use of a _____ .

h. An undertaker would direct plans for a _____ .

i. An environmentalist would work to keep the surroundings _____ .

j. A gem collector would deal in _____ .

k. An automobile assembly-line worker would be involved with _____ .

l. A mystery writer would develop stories that deal in _____ .

VII. Crossword Puzzle. Solve the puzzle by using words from the spelling list. Check your answers in the **Glossary/SPELLEX®**.

Across

2. honest
4. to present someone to another
8. to be part of a total

Down

1. dark and dim
3. not polite
5. finished
6. causing pain
7. to lessen

VIII. All in a Sentence.

Use all of the spelling words or **Other Word Forms** (p. 43) to write two short articles about the following subjects. Use each spelling word only once between the two articles. Circle the spelling words and the other word forms you used.

The Loss of a Pet

Example: *The* (funeral) (included) *one brief speech by a friend.*

Pets play significant roles in the lives of many Americans, often taking the place of spouses, children, and friends. The loss of a pet can be a grief-filled, emotional experience. Owners mourning the loss of beloved pets often select pet cemeteries to lay their "animal friends" to rest.

According to the International Pet Cemetery Association, there are 400 registered pet cemeteries in the United States, some dating back to the 1800's. Today more and more Americans are choosing pet cemeteries as the final resting places for their pets. Pet cemeteries have gained in favor because society has come to accept the fact that grieving for a deceased pet is not an oddball behavior.

New regulations have been set up by the International Pet Cemetery Association to assure that pet cemetery owners maintain quality standards. Pet cemeteries must be constructed on dedicated land, land that can be used only as cemeteries. Pet cemeteries must measure at least five acres in size. And, owners of pet cemeteries must set aside funds to provide perpetual care for the cemetery grounds.

The average pet burial with a plot of land, tombstone, and small casket costs about $250. Many feel this is a small price to pay for a pet's loyalty and devotion.

How to Manufacture Rings at Low Cost

Example: *The new machine* (reduces) *the need for extra employees.*

On Friday, Samuel Simpson, president of the Simpson Emblem and Ring Company, unveiled a revolutionary plan for manufacturing low-cost rings. The plan was introduced at the company's annual stockholder meeting held at the Blake House Inn. Two hundred stockholders and managers attended the all-day session to hear Simpson's plan for long-term growth.

The major thrust of the Simpson plan includes investment in a computerized, metal-processing machine that transforms small metal ingots into intricately shaped rings in minutes, eliminating the traditional use of casts and time-consuming procedures. The machine was designed by Edward Muller and Thomas Ender, long-time employees at the Simpson Research Center.

According to Simpson, adoption of the plan will require a reorganization of several departments at the processing plant on Halston Road. The computerized procedure will reduce the need for an estimated 100 employees at the processing plant. Union officials have been advised of the unemployment potential and are presently working with management to address the reduction problems that will result for the workers.

Simpson assured the stockholders and managers present that the interests of the employees are priority with the management. "Though the plan brings with it both good news and bad news," he commented at the conclusion of his remarks, "I promise that the bad news will become good news during the transition process. The workers will not be abandoned."

IX. Final Test. Write each spelling word.

1	2	3	4	5
raisin	thief	squeeze	tournament	groceries
shoulder	medicine	overflow	jewels	unpack
salute	notice	screwdriver	unwise	entertain
musical	exclaim	excitement	rascal	manual
umpire	obey	convince	agreement	polite

I. Cause and Effect. Use other word forms or the spelling words to complete the sentences. The number tells you in what column you can find the spelling word. If you need help, use the **Glossary/SPELLEX®**.

a. Because I _____ the box, the _____ were crushed.
   ₃ ₁

b. Because the _____ bag was too full, it _____ .
   ₅ ₃

c. Because a band of _____ stole the basketballs, all _____
   ₂ ₄
   were canceled.

d. Because the doctor _____ the boxes quickly, the _____
   ₅ ₂
   were saved.

e. Because the officer's _____ were broken, _____ the
   ₁ ₁
   general was impossible.

f. Because one _____ in the band was late, the _____
   ₁ ₅
   was postponed.

g. Because the company's _____ were outdated, the newest
   ₅
   _____ were not illustrated.
   ₃

h. Because you found the _____ , I cheered _____ .
   ₄ ₃

i. Because I acted _____ , I was called a _____ .
   ₄ ₄

j. Because they _____ my weight loss, my parents _____ ,
   ₂ ₂
   "Well done!"

k. Because the children _____ to behave, they _____
   ₄ ₃
   the teacher to let them read together.

l. Because the game was rained out, all the _____ went home.
   ₁

m. Because you behaved _____ , I thanked you _____ .
   ₂ ₅

47

12

	1	2	3	4	5
	mass	raid	claims	explain	contain
	machinery	speech	photograph	received	nowhere
	dislike	admire	cruel	greater	private
	foreign	niece	poultry	neither	introduce
	arrive	total	through	adventure	tour

II. Newspaper Headlines. Use other word forms or the spelling words to complete the headlines. The number tells you in what column you can find the spelling word. Capitalize each word. If you need help, use the **Glossary/SPELLEX®**.

a. Giant Ants _____ Picnic Last Night

2

b. Agitated Washing _____ Overflow

1

c. _____ Farmers Scramble for Egg Business

3

d. Sea _____ Promise Whale of a Good Time

4

e. Jars _____ Peanut Butter Missing From Shelves

5

f. Students' _____ Heard Today

2

g. Prevent _____ to Animals Week Planned

3

h. Dog _____ Leash

1

i. Santa's Elves Meet _____ to Discuss Wages

5

j. Nephews and _____ Search for Aunts and Uncles

2

k. Trapeze Artist _____ for Hands and Feats

2

l. Jack _____ Award for Climbing Bean Stalk

4

m. Collectors Display _____ Stamps

1

n. Cinderella _____ Glass Footwear

5

o. Denmark's Ruler Considered _____ Dane

4

p. Doctors _____ Cure for Common Cold

3

q. Train Finally _____ on Time

1

r. Trips to _____ Advertised by Travel Agent

5

s. Facts Reveal _____ Hansel Nor Gretel Liked Gingerbread

4

t. Alice Reports Hare-raising Journey _____ Looking Glass

3

u. Number of Dwarfs Found Whistling in Woods _____ Seven

2

v. _____ Class Plans Exhibit

3

w. _____ Through Haunted Castles May Lift Spirits

5

x. Scientist _____ Why People Slurp

4

y. _____ of People Jam Phone Booth

1

1	2	3	4	5
advice	exact	inquire	needless	reduce
bargain	glory	journey	noble	rude
brief	grief	margin	normal	standard
decline	horizon	minor	proceed	truthful
energy	important	natural	proof	vain

III. Break the Code. Use the code to write an other word form for each spelling word. Write each word.

a	b	c	d	e	f	g	h	i	j	k	l	m
↕	↕	↕	↕	↕	↕	↕	↕	↕	↕	↕	↕	↕
z	y	x	w	v	u	t	s	r	q	p	o	n

a. vczxgob

b. mlyovhg

c. nrmlih

d. nzitrmzo

e. tolirurvh

f. ivwfxvw

g. mlinzoob

h. ezmrgb

i. yzitzrmvw

j. qlfimvbh

k. vmvitvgrx

l. wvxormrmt

m. mzgfivh

n. ifwvob

o. sliralmgzo

p. zwerhvw

q. yirvuob

r. rmjfrivh

s. kilevm

t. hgzmwziwh

u. tirvev

v. gifgsufoob

w. mvvwovhhob

x. kilxvvwrmt

y. rnkligzmxv

12

1	2	3	4	5
attain	desire	include	pier	source
chamber	entirely	manufacturing	porter	staff
continent	funeral	motion	primary	steer
contribute	gloomy	obtain	produce	uncertain
creep	inclined	peer	silent	weekly

IV. Word Arithmetic. Perform one or two operations on each spelling word to write an other word form.

a. creep + s = _____

b. source + s = _____

c. obtain + ing = _____

d. silent + ly = _____

e. funeral + s = _____

f. peer + ed = _____

g. attain + ing = _____

h. uncertain + ty = _____

i. desire + s = _____

j. porter + s = _____

k. produce + s = _____

l. contribute + s = _____

m. chamber + ed = _____

n. manufacturing – ing + ed = _____

o. steer + ing = _____

p. weekly – ly = _____

q. gloomy – y = _____

r. pier + s = _____

s. motion + ed = _____

t. staff + ing = _____

u. primary – y + ies = _____

v. inclined – ed + ing = _____

w. continent + al = _____

x. entirely – ly + ty = _____

y. include – e + ing = _____

Lesson 13

I. Check Test. Write each spelling word.

II. Spelling Words and Phrases

acre	**acre** of swampland
labor	new **labor** unions
major	**major** effort
flavor	an improved **flavor**
favorite	**favorite** color
capable	**capable** carpenter
dangerous	a **dangerous** adventure
stranger	a total **stranger**
exchange	will **exchange** a shirt
arrangement	flower **arrangement**
invitation	**invitation** to lunch
operation	a minor **operation**
observation	**observation** tower
radiation	the sun's **radiation**
transportation	public **transportation**
stationary	a **stationary** target
area	picnic **area**
solo	**solo** flight
echo	hollow **echo**
volcano	erupting **volcano**

III. Find a Fit. Write each word in its correct shape.

a. ☐☐☐☐
b. ☐☐☐☐
c. ☐☐☐☐
d. ☐☐☐☐
e. ☐☐☐☐☐
f. ☐☐☐☐☐☐
g. ☐☐☐☐☐
h. ☐☐☐☐☐☐
i. ☐☐☐☐☐☐
j. ☐☐☐☐☐☐☐☐☐
k. ☐☐☐☐☐☐☐☐☐
l. ☐☐☐☐☐☐☐
m. ☐☐☐☐☐☐☐☐
n. ☐☐☐☐☐☐☐☐☐☐
o. ☐☐☐☐☐☐☐
p. ☐☐☐☐☐☐
q. ☐☐☐☐☐☐☐☐
r. ☐☐☐☐☐☐
s. ☐☐☐☐☐☐☐
t. ☐☐☐☐☐☐☐☐

Other Word Forms
acres, acreage, labored, laboring, laborer, majored, majority, flavors, flavorful, favor, favoring, capably, danger, dangerously, strange, strangely, strangeness, exchanged, exchanging, arrange, arranges, arranging, invited, inviting, operate, operating, operations, operator, observe, observant, radiate, radiating, transport, transported, areas, solos, soloist, echoes, volcanoes, volcanic

51

IV. Crossword Puzzle. Solve the puzzle by using all the words from the spelling list. Check your answers in the **Glossary/SPELLEX®**.

Across
1. to give a taste to
4. a repeated sound
7. unsafe
9. a flat, open space
10. an unknown person
11. work
12. an army officer
13. a heart transplant
16. a fiery mountain
17. a request to attend a party
18. something seen

Down
1. best-liked
2. the process of giving off energy
3. able
4. to trade for something else
5. planes, buses, and trains
6. the way something is put in order
8. not moving
14. a measure of land
15. alone

Spelling Words

acre labor major flavor favorite capable dangerous stranger exchange arrangement invitation operation observation radiation transportation stationary area solo echo volcano

V. Guide Words. The word pairs are guide words from the **Glossary/SPELLEX®**. Write the words from the spelling list that appear on the same page as each pair of guide words.

Example:

desire—document

_____ *destroy*

_____ *distant*

abandon—adventure

1. _____

advertise—assign

2. _____

3. _____

boiler—chalk

4. _____

customer—design

5. _____

doubt—estate

6. _____

evil—fault

7. _____

favor—future

8. _____

9. _____

insects—knowledge

10. _____

labor—machine

11. _____

machinery—mining

12. _____

obey—percent

13. _____

14. _____

punctual—refuse

15. _____

silent—staff

16. _____

standard—succeed

17. _____

18. _____

theater—treat

19. _____

vary—wrench

20. _____

VI. Writing Sentences. Write each set of words in a sentence. You may use **Other Word Forms** (p. 51).

1. capable—dangerous—operation

2. flavor—favorite—observation

3. solo—stranger—labor

4. major—volcano—acre

5. radiation—area—echo

6. invitation—arrangement—exchange

7. stationary—transportation

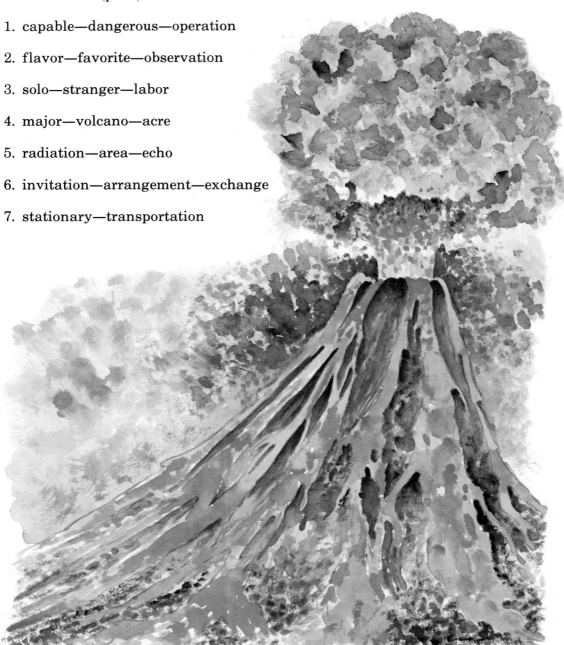

VII. Final Test. Write each spelling word.

Lesson 14

I. Check Test. Write each spelling word.

II. Spelling Words and Phrases

plank	an oak **plank**
sprang	**sprang** higher
scratch	won't **scratch** the itch
scramble	had to **scramble** down
glance	a **glance** backward
advance	**advance** notice
balance	will **balance** the scales
damage	free from **damage**
manage	will **manage** to finish
command	giving a **command**
gallop	began to **gallop**
wrapped	was **wrapped** in foil
planned	**planned** a picnic
manner	a careful **manner**
scatter	will **scatter** seeds
frankly	**frankly** speaking
lasting	**lasting** friendship
landlord	paid the **landlord**
practice	to **practice** the piano
plunge	will **plunge** into water

III. Find a Fit. Write each word in its correct shape.

a.
b.
c.
d.
e.
f.
g.
h.
i.
j.
k.
l.
m.
n.
o.
p.
q.
r.
s.
t.

Other Word Forms

planks, spring, sprung, scratched, scratching, scrambled, scrambling, glanced, glancing, advanced, advancing, balanced, balancing, damaged, damaging, managed, managing, commanded, commanding, galloped, galloping, wrap, wrapped, wrapping, plan, planning, mannered, scattered, scattering, frank, frankest, last, lasted, landlords, practiced, practicing, practically, plunged, plunging

IV. All in a Row.
Write the twenty spelling words in alphabetical order. Then join the boxed letters and write four hidden words.

1. __ __ ☐ __ __ __ __
2. __ ☐ __ __ ☐ __ __
3. __ __ __ __ __ __ ☐
4. __ ☐ __ __ __ __
5. __ __ __ __ __ ☐ __

Hidden Word: _____

11. ☐ __ __ __ __ __
12. __ __ ☐ __ __ __
13. __ __ __ ☐ __ __ __ __
14. __ __ __ ☐ __ ☐ __
15. __ ☐ __ __ __ __ __ __

Hidden Word: _____

6. __ __ __ __ ☐ ☐
7. __ __ __ __ __ ☐
8. __ __ ☐ __ __ __ __ __
9. __ __ __ ☐ __ __
10. __ __ ☐ __ ☐ __

Hidden Word: _____

16. ☐ __ __ __ __ __ __
17. __ ☐ __ __ __ __ __
18. __ __ ☐ __ __ __ __
19. __ __ __ ☐ __ __ __
20. __ __ __ ☐ __ ☐ __

Hidden Word: _____

V. Word Building.
The words below can all be used as verbs. Add suffixes to build new words. Write the words.

Base Words	*ed* Words	*ing* Words
a. scratch	_____	_____
b. plunge	_____	_____
c. plan	_____	_____
d. glance	_____	_____
e. advance	_____	_____
f. balance	_____	_____
g. damage	_____	_____
h. manage	_____	_____
i. scramble	_____	_____
j. command	_____	_____
k. scatter	_____	_____
l. gallop	_____	_____
m. practice	_____	_____
n. wrap	_____	_____

Spelling Words

plank   sprang   scratch   scramble   glance   advance   balance
damage   manage   command   gallop   wrapped   planned
manner   scatter   frankly   lasting   landlord   practice   plunge

VI. Finding Words. The words in the spelling list appear in the beginning (A-H), middle (I-Q), or end (R-Z) of the **Glossary/SPELLEX®**. Write each word.

Beginning A-H	Middle I-Q	End R-Z
1. _____	1. _____	1. _____
2. _____	2. _____	2. _____
3. _____	3. _____	3. _____
4. _____	4. _____	4. _____
5. _____	5. _____	5. _____
6. _____	6. _____	
7. _____	7. _____	
	8. _____	

VII. Generally Speaking. Write a spelling word in the group it best fits.

    a. continuing, remaining, _____

    b. leaped, jumped, _____

    c. way, style, _____

    d. board, lumber, _____

    e. renter, owner, _____

    f. openly, honestly, _____

VIII. Building Sentences. Write the following phrases in sentences.

    a. does <u>command</u> the army

    b. to <u>damage</u> the car

    c. will <u>gallop</u> away

    d. sudden <u>advance</u>

    e. new <u>landlord</u>

    f. expressed herself <u>frankly</u>

    g. hours of <u>practice</u>

    h. strange <u>manner</u>

    i. off <u>balance</u>

    j. a deep <u>plunge</u>

    k. broken <u>plank</u>

    l. <u>planned</u> an escape

    m. couldn't <u>scramble</u> over

    n. will <u>scatter</u> seeds

    o. to <u>glance</u> down the street

    p. <u>sprang</u> up

    q. <u>wrapped</u> around

    r. might <u>scratch</u> the table

    s. couldn't <u>manage</u>

    t. was <u>lasting</u>

IX. Final Test. Write each spelling word.

I. Check Test. Write each spelling word.

II. Spelling Words and Phrases

weave	to spin and **weave**
league	a minor **league** team
breathe	to **breathe** deeply
speaker	today's **speaker**
creature	a weird **creature**
treatment	silent **treatment**
defeat	a win or a **defeat**
retreat	will **retreat** from danger
beneath	**beneath** the sea
appeal	an **appeal** for help
disease	a **disease** spread by fleas
release	can **release** the balloon
increase	an **increase** in allowance
theater	a movie **theater**
realizes	**realizes** they're lazy
meant	**meant** no harm
measure	a teaspoon **measure**
pleasure	a **pleasure** to serve you
jealous	a **jealous** student
search	to **search** the beach

III. Find a Fit. Write each word in its correct shape.

a.

b.

c.

d.

e.

f.

g.

h.

i.

j.

k.

l.

m.

n.

o.

p.

q.

r.

s.

t.

Other Word Forms

weaved, weaving, leagues, breathes, breathed, breathing, speak, spoke, speech, creatures, treat, treatments, defeated, defeating, retreated, retreating, appealing, diseased, released, releasing, increased, increasing, theaters, realize, realizing, realization, mean, meaning, measures, measured, measuring, pleasures, pleasurable, jealousy, searches, searching

IV. Sort Your Words. Each of the words in the spelling list has an *ea* combination. Write the spelling words in the correct boxes.

Words With a Long *e* Sound		Words With a Short *e* Sound
1. _____	9. _____	1. _____
2. _____	10. _____	2. _____
3. _____	11. _____	3. _____
4. _____	12. _____	4. _____
5. _____	13. _____	
6. _____	14. _____	
7. _____	15. _____	
8. _____		

Write the one word in which the vowel sound is *r*-controlled. _____

V. Guide Words. These word pairs are guide words from the **Glossary/SPELLEX®.** Write the words from the spelling list that appear on the same page as each pair of guide words.

advertise—assign
1. _____

assigned—boil
2. _____

boiler—chalk
3. _____

concern—cushion
4. _____

customer—design
5. _____

desire—document
6. _____

hesitate—insect
7. _____

insects—knowledge
8. _____

labor—machine
9. _____

machinery—mining
10. _____
11. _____

perform—poultry
12. _____

punctual—refuse
13. _____

regard—scarce
14. _____
15. _____

scarcely—sicken
16. _____

silent—staff
17. _____

theater—treat
18. _____

treatment—various
19. _____

vary—wrench
20. _____

Spelling Words

weave   league   breathe   speaker   creature   treatment   defeat
retreat   beneath   appeal   disease   release   increase   theater
realizes   meant   measure   pleasure   jealous   search

VI. Be a Sentence Detective. Unscramble the word under each blank. Write each unscrambled word.

a. The senator made an _____ for an _____ in taxes.
    leappa   crinsaee

b. I _____ to sign up for the bowling _____ yesterday.
    aemnt   ueglae

c. The angry _____ made a demand for the immediate
    keespar
_____ of the prisoners.
    reelsea

d. The doctor thought the _____ would cure the _____ .
    teamnttre   seedsia

e. _____ the apple tree we could _____ in the sweet odors.
    theenab   theeabr

f. The monstrous _____ was _____ of its rival.
    trueeacr   aejouls

g. When an army _____ it is losing, it plans a _____ .
    zealsier   ateertr

h. Be sure to _____ your amount of wool before you _____
    seemaur   veewa
on the loom.

i. The baby-sitter was making a _____ for things to give
    rcheas
_____ to the children.
    seeauplr

j. The movie in the _____ showed the hero overcoming a recent
    tearthe
_____ .
    tafede

VII. All in a Sentence.
Use all of the spelling words or **Other Word Forms** (p. 59) to write two short articles with the following titles. Use each spelling word only once between the two articles. Circle the spelling words and the other word forms you used.

Alone, Pursued, Rescued

Example: *When the ⟨search⟩ finally ended, I ⟨breathed⟩ a sigh of relief.*

Captain Lloyd Roberts, the long-lost pilot of Central Air Lines, was found alive on Saturday morning as he wandered into a small village on the outskirts of Hope Valley. Roberts had been missing, and feared dead, since October when his single-engine plane disappeared mysteriously while flying over the rain forests of western Brazil. Roberts was the sole occupant of the plane.

According to reports, Roberts appeared dazed and weakened from the experience. He told of a violent electrical storm occurring before the crash. Though the actual cause of the crash is still not known, authorities are trying to piece together the ordeal of his miraculous survival.

It appears that Roberts wandered for days after the crash before sighting any sign of human life. He was pursued by unfriendly natives for days and eventually escaped by swimming beside a dugout he found abandoned on the banks of a river. Roberts was finally rescued by a party of engineers exploring the Amazon area by boat.

Exhausted and ill with fever, Roberts is reported to have said "Please let my family know I'm safe. Then they can stop worrying about me and get on with their lives."

Arrangements are now underway to fly Roberts back to the states.

The Contest

Example: *This year the number of participants has ⟨increased.⟩*

Two hundred sixth graders in the area's public and private schools will compete in an unusual contest next week. The contest will include six events ranging from pie eating to tests of historical trivia. The purpose of each event is to draw public attention to the importance of READING as a tool for learning.

It is estimated that 18% of the adult population in Pineville County cannot read simple text. The sixth graders find that percentage to be alarmingly high and want the figure reduced. Proceeds from the six competitive events will be donated to the Literacy Council of Pineville County for their developmental reading programs. According to Tom Farr, sixth-grade organizer of the contests, "To reduce the problem of illiteracy, you must first make the public aware of the problem. And that's what the sixth graders of Pineville County intend to do!"

The contest is sponsored by the Shoppers' Village Mall at Kendall Square. The events are scheduled to be held in the mall auditorium at 5:00 P.M., Monday through Friday of next week. Come on down and lend your support to the sixth graders of Pineville County.

VIII. Final Test.
Write each spelling word.

Lesson 16

I. Check Test. Write each spelling word.

II. Spelling Words and Phrases

highly	**highly** explosive
slight	a **slight** error
frighten	couldn't **frighten** me
delightfully	a **delightfully** cool breeze
twilight	**twilight** shadows
height	**height** of eight feet
diameter	**diameter** of the circle
bicycle	the stolen **bicycle**
design	to draw a **design**
satisfied	a **satisfied** customer
stylish	**stylish** suit
typewriter	**typewriter** keyboard
rinse	to **rinse** or wash
width	narrow **width**
midst	**midst** the crowd
knitting	**knitting** and sewing
trimmed	cut and **trimmed**
slither	to **slither** away
system	computer **system**
mystery	weird **mystery** story

III. Find a Fit. Write each word in its correct shape.

a.

b.

c.

d.

e.

f.

g.

h.

i.

j.

k.

l.

m.

n.

o.

p.

q.

r.

s.

t.

Other Word Forms

high, highest, slightly, slightest, fright, frightened, frightening, delight, delighted, delightful, twilights, heights, diameters, bicycles, bicycling, designed, designer, satisfy, satisfies, satisfying, satisfaction, style, styling, stylishly, typewriters, typewritten, rinsed, rinsing, widths, mid, middle, knit, knitted, trim, trimming, slithers, slithered, slithering, systems, mysteries, mysterious

63

IV. The *I*'s Have It. All the spelling words have either a long or a short *i* sound. Write each spelling word in the correct box. A word may go in more than one box.

Short *i* Sound

Spelled *i*

1. _____
2. _____
3. _____
4. _____
5. _____
6. _____
7. _____
8. _____

Spelled *y*

1. _____
2. _____
3. _____

Spelled *e*

1. _____
2. _____
3. _____

Long *i* Sound

Spelled *i*

1. _____
2. _____
3. _____
4. _____
5. _____
6. _____
7. _____
8. _____
9. _____

Spelled *y*

1. _____
2. _____

Spelled *ei*

1. _____

Spelled *ie*

1. _____

V. Phrase Clues. Use a spelling word to complete each phrase.

a. _____ needles

b. solved the _____

c. _____ suspicious

d. length and _____

e. electric _____

f. _____ and weight

g. traced the _____

h. didn't _____ me

i. a _____ coat

j. _____ his beard

k. _____ their hunger

l. in the _____ of the crowd

m. only a _____ breeze

n. long shadows of _____

o. a _____ refreshing swim

p. will _____ the dishes

q. _____ of the circle

r. rode on the _____ path

s. a communications _____

t. did _____ across the road

Spelling Words

highly slight frighten delightfully twilight height
diameter bicycle design satisfied stylish typewriter rinse
width midst knitting trimmed slither system mystery

VI. Break the Code. Use the code to write the spelling words.

a	b	c	d	e	f	g	h	i	j	k	l	m	n	o	p	q	r	s	t	u	v	w	x	y	z
↓	↓	↓	↓	↓	↓	↓	↓	↓	↓	↓	↓	↓	↓	↓	↓	↓	↓	↓	↓	↓	↓	↓	↓	↓	↓
g	d	z	r	u	e	y	w	k	a	c	p	s	h	b	n	l	m	f	v	t	x	q	o	j	i

a. nfzanu _____

b. bfmzap _____

c. bfqzanuseqqg _____

d. uhzqzanu _____

e. mqzanu _____

f. sdzanufp _____

g. bzjrfufd _____

h. ozkgkqf _____

i. rgmufdg _____

j. rzbmu _____

k. hzbun _____

l. udzrrfb _____

m. mqzunfd _____

n. mjuzmszfb _____

o. mgmufr _____

p. mugqzmn _____

q. ipzuuzpa _____

r. nzanqg _____

s. uglfhdzufd _____

t. dzpmf _____

VII. Be a Word Doctor. Write the one operation you must perform before adding the suffix to each word. Write the new word.

	Operations		New Words
Example: skim	_double the_ m	+ ed =	_skimmed_
a. mystery	_____	+ ous =	_____
b. trim	_____	+ ed =	_____
c. knit	_____	+ ing =	_____
d. typewrite	_____	+ er =	_____
e. style	_____	+ ish =	_____
f. satisfy	_____	+ ed =	_____
g. bicycle	_____	+ ing =	_____
h. rinse	_____	+ ing =	_____

VIII. Rewriting as Questions. Rewrite these sentences as questions.

a. They can <u>design</u> a new heating <u>system</u>.

b. You will <u>rinse</u> your socks.

c. She should stand to her fullest <u>height</u>.

d. The child will play the music <u>delightfully</u>.

e. The teacher will want the paper <u>trimmed</u> to a very narrow <u>width</u>.

f. Its sudden disappearance in the <u>midst</u> of the crowd was a <u>mystery</u>.

g. You are considered <u>highly</u> <u>stylish</u>.

h. They will <u>frighten</u> easily.

i. We can measure the <u>diameter</u> of the volleyball.

j. They will <u>slither</u> down the muddy slope.

k. There was a <u>slight</u> noise a few seconds later.

l. He was <u>satisfied</u> with the <u>typewriter</u>.

m. My friend was out riding the <u>bicycle</u> until <u>twilight</u>.

n. My cousin is <u>knitting</u> mittens for us.

IX. Final Test. Write each spelling word.

Lesson 17

I. Check Test. Write each spelling word.

II. Spelling Words and Phrases

term	school **term**
nerve	the **nerve** to try
serve	a poor **serve**
servant	hired another **servant**
permanent	left a **permanent** mark
personal	**personal** belongings
deserve	**deserve** one more chance
dessert	fruit for **dessert**
reverse	can **reverse** the order
terror	filled with **terror**
territory	the animal's **territory**
terrible	**terrible** mistake
berry	a nut or a **berry**
buried	**buried** in the garden
computer	**computer** programmer
curve	**curve** in the road
furnace	a hot **furnace**
surface	swam to the **surface**
purchase	will **purchase** a gift
purpose	forgot the **purpose**

III. Find a Fit. Write each word in its correct shape.

a.
b.
c.
d.
e.
f.
g.
h.
i.
j.
k.
l.
m.
n.
o.
p.
q.
r.
s.
t.

Other Word Forms

terms, termed, nerves, nervous, serves, served, serving, servants, permanently, person, personally, personality, deserves, deserved, deserving, desserts, reverses, reversing, reversal, terrors, territories, territorial, terribly, berries, bury, buries, burying, compute, computers, curves, curved, curving, furnaces, surfaces, surfacing, purchases, purchased, purchasing, purposes, purposely, purposeful

IV. *Er or Ur.* The letters *er* and *ur* often have the same sound. List the spelling words in alphabetical order. Put a wavy line under the words spelled with *er*. Circle the words spelled with *ur*. Put an **X** before the five words in which *er* does not have the sound as in *burn* or *fern*.

1. _____   8. _____   15. _____
2. _____   9. _____   16. _____
3. _____   10. _____   17. _____
4. _____   11. _____   18. _____
5. _____   12. _____   19. _____
6. _____   13. _____   20. _____
7. _____   14. _____

V. Generally Speaking. Write each of the spelling words in the group it best fits.

a. area, region, _____

b. arc, bend, _____

c. butler, maid, _____

d. length of time, school session, _____

e. ice cream, pie, _____

f. sell, buy, _____

g. machine, calculator, _____

h. fear, horror, _____

i. stove, heater, _____

j. awful, bad, _____

k. earn, worthy of, _____

l. fruit, grape, _____

m. reason, goal, _____

n. covered, put under, _____

o. courage, strong will, _____

p. lasting, won't wear out, _____

q. change direction, backward, _____

r. wait on, work for, _____

s. rise to the top, outside layer, _____

t. private, one's own, _____

Spelling Words

term nerve serve servant permanent personal deserve dessert reverse terror territory terrible berry buried computer curve furnace surface purchase purpose

VI. Finding Words. The words in the spelling list appear in the beginning (A-H), middle (I-Q), or end (R-Z) of the **Glossary/SPELLEX®.** Write each word.

Beginning A-H	Middle I-Q	End R-Z
1. _____	1. _____	1. _____
2. _____	2. _____	2. _____
3. _____	3. _____	3. _____
4. _____	4. _____	4. _____
5. _____	5. _____	5. _____
6. _____		6. _____
7. _____		7. _____
		8. _____

VII. Hidden Words. Read each sentence to find clues to the hidden spelling words. Circle the word hidden in each set of underlined words. Write each word.

a. The poet changed direction and wrote <u>more verse</u>. _____

b. This school <u>semester may</u> be my last. _____

c. That <u>person always</u> deals with private matters. _____

d. Winding <u>paths</u> don't <u>occur very</u> often. _____

e. The brave <u>runner veered</u> into the traffic to save the child. _____

VIII. All in a Sentence. Use each of the spelling words in sentences about one of the following titles. You may use **Other Word Forms** (p. 67). Circle the spelling words and the other word forms you used.

<u>A Long Walk Back</u> or <u>Just One More Time</u>

IX. Final Test. Write each spelling word.

1	2	3	4	5
frighten	bicycle	stranger	echo	mystery
dangerous	bury	breathe	terror	area
scratch	scramble	slither	search	observation
plunge	territory	planned	creature	height
realizes	measure	reverse	deserve	sprang

I. Story Time. Write other word forms or the spelling words to complete the sentences. The number tells you in what column you can find the spelling word. Write each word or its other word form only once. If you need help, use the **Glossary/SPELLEX®**.

The Buried Treasure

One day after school, we found two (a) _____ notes left on our (5)

(b) _____ . The notes told us where to find (c) _____ (2)
treasure. Immediately, we pedaled off to the mountain, the first of the two

(d) _____ described in the notes. We felt a bit (e) _____ (5)
wondering what (f) _____ lay ahead. (1)

From the mountaintop, we (g) _____ the sun going down. Though not (5)
usually afraid of (h) _____ , we were indeed frightened by the (5)

(i) _____ of the area. Then we heard a voice that shrieked and (3)

(j) _____ . We went (k) _____ to our feet, and then we (4)
(5)

(l) _____ down the mountain to the valley. (2)

After (m) _____ an itch on my foot, I (n) _____ into a (1)
pool of cold water and lost my (o) _____ . After this brief moment of (3)

(p) _____ , I (q) _____ that I still wanted to keep (4)
(1)

(r) _____ for the marked (s) _____ . (4)
(2)

Suddenly, several furry (t) _____ that (u) _____ eight feet (4)
(2)
in height stood in our way. Trembling, we crouched down and (v) _____ (3)
through the grass, changing our (w) _____ and (x) _____ (3)
(3)
our direction.

To our surprise, we backed into the two sticks marking the buried treasure. After our long search, we felt we (y) _____ the treasure. (4)

18

1	2	3	4	5
wrapped	plank	operation	dessert	acre
servant	invitation	speaker	practice	trimmed
solo	theater	furnace	meant	league
beneath	design	midst	knitting	gallop
typewriter	purchase	manner	volcano	computer

II. Out of the Ordinary Days. Complete each title by writing other word forms or the spelling words. The number tells you in what column you can find the spelling word. Capitalize each word.

Example: Present (1) ___*Wrapping*___ Day

a. Plow Forty (5) _____ Day

b. Hair (5) _____ Day

c. (3) _____ on a Doctor Day

d. (1) _____ One Helping of Vegetables Day

e. Eat Delicious (4) _____ Day

f. Spare All Bowling (5) _____ Day

g. Wear Earmuffs on Guest (3) _____ Day

h. Forget (4) _____ the Piano Day

i. Nail the (2) _____ Together Day

j. (2) _____ a Pet to Dinner Day

k. Sing Two (1) _____ in the Shower Day

l. Ride (5) _____ Horses Day

m. Hide (1) _____ the Stairs Day

n. Visit Four Movie (2) _____ Day

o. Say What You (4) _____ Day

p. Tap on Ten Tiny (1) _____ Day

q. Buy Needles for (4) _____ Day

r. Fix Flaming (3) _____ Day

s. Debug All (5) _____ Day

t. Eat Only the (3) _____ of Your Sandwich Day

u. Draw Dotted (2) _____ Day

v. View a (4) _____ Eruption Day

w. Mind Your (3) _____ Day

x. Return Unwanted (2) _____ Day

1	2	3	4	5
favorite	arrangement	radiation	transportation	flavor
command	balance	advance	damage	manage
treatment	retreat	defeat	appeal	weave
satisfied	delightfully	stylish	width	highly
curve	surface	purpose	terrible	serve

III. Word Building. Add word parts to each spelling word or its base word to make other word forms. If you need help, use the **Glossary/SPELLEX®**.

Spelling Words	s or es	ed	ing
Example: wave	*waves*	*waved*	*waving*
a. flavor			
b. command			
c. balance			
d. retreat			
e. damage			
f. favorite	*favors*		
g. arrangement			
h. radiation			
i. transportation			
j. manage			
k. treatment			*treating*
l. advance			
m. defeat			
n. appeal			
o. weave			
p. delightfully			
q. stylish			
r. curve			
s. surface			
t. serve			
u. satisfied			
v. purpose			
w. width			

Write two other word forms for each spelling word below.

highly _____ _____

terrible _____ _____

18

1	2	3	4	5
major	labor	capable	exchange	stationary
frankly	lasting	glance	scatter	landlord
disease	increase	release	pleasure	jealous
slight	twilight	diameter	system	rinse
term	nerve	buried	permanent	personal

IV. Words in a Series. Use other word forms or the spelling words to complete each series. The number tells you in what column you can find the spelling word. Use each word or its other word form only once.

a. working, toiling, (2) _____

b. trading, swapping, (4) _____

c. unmoving, motionless, (5) _____

d. captains, colonels, (1) _____

e. exists, continues, (2) _____

f. able, qualified, (3) _____

g. sprinkling, throwing about, (4) _____

h. gaining, growing, (2) _____

i. owners, renters, (5) _____

j. envy, suspicion, (5) _____

k. sincere, truthful, (1) _____

l. delights, joys, (4) _____

m. dusk, nightfall, (2) _____

n. washing lightly, spraying, (5) _____

o. looking, staring, (3) _____

p. methods, plans, (4) _____

q. untied, freed, (3) _____

r. sicknesses, ailments, (1) _____

s. circle, radius, (3) _____

t. lastingly, enduringly, (4) _____

u. least, smallest, (1) _____

v. times, school periods, (1) _____

w. hide, cover up, (3) _____

x. courageous, brave, (2) _____

y. individual, human being, (5) _____

Lesson 19

I. Check Test. Write each spelling word.

II. Spelling Words and Phrases

spare	a **spare** tire
stare	will dare you to **stare**
carefully	**carefully** wrapped
warehouse	a stocked **warehouse**
declare	may **declare** war
prepare	to **prepare** a report
farewell	said their **farewell**
scarcely	**scarcely** aware
various	in **various** stages
armor	the knight's **armor**
article	a newspaper **article**
argument	a no-win **argument**
starve	would rather **starve**
garbage	**garbage** collection
charming	a **charming** manner
regard	without **regard**
department	the art **department**
charity	**charity** work
sheriff	deputy **sheriff**
favorable	a **favorable** choice

III. Find a Fit. Write each word in its correct shape.

a.
b.
c.
d.
e.
f.
g.
h.
i.
j.
k.
l.
m.
n.
o.
p.
q.
r.
s.
t.

Other Word Forms

spared, sparing, sparingly, stares, staring, care, careful, warehouses, declared, declaring, declaration, prepared, preparing, preparation, farewells, scarce, scarcity, vary, varying, armors, armory, articles, argue, argued, arguing, starves, starving, starvation, charm, charmed, regards, regarded, departments, departmental, charities, sheriffs, favor, favorite

IV. StARt to StARe. Eighteen spelling words have an *ar* combination. Write each *ar* spelling word in the correct box.

ar as in *far*		ar as in *fare* or *carry*	
1. _____		1. _____	6. _____
2. _____		2. _____	7. _____
3. _____		3. _____	8. _____
4. _____		4. _____	9. _____
5. _____		5. _____	10. _____
6. _____			
7. _____			
8. _____			

Write the two words that did not fit in either box.

    1. _____   2. _____

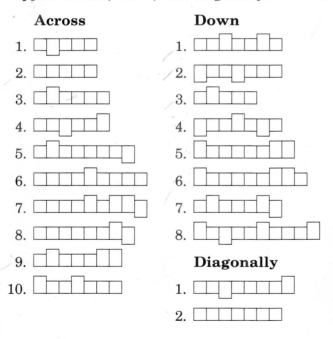

V. Hide and Seek. The spelling words can be found in the word puzzle. The words appear across, down, and diagonally. Circle and write the words.

Across

1. ☐☐☐☐
2. ☐☐☐☐☐
3. ☐☐☐☐☐
4. ☐☐☐☐☐
5. ☐☐☐☐☐☐
6. ☐☐☐☐☐☐☐
7. ☐☐☐☐☐☐☐
8. ☐☐☐☐☐☐
9. ☐☐☐☐☐
10. ☐☐☐☐☐

Down

1. ☐☐☐☐☐☐
2. ☐☐☐☐☐☐
3. ☐☐☐☐
4. ☐☐☐☐☐
5. ☐☐☐☐☐☐
6. ☐☐☐☐☐☐☐
7. ☐☐☐☐☐☐
8. ☐☐☐☐☐☐☐

Diagonally

1. ☐☐☐☐☐☐
2. ☐☐☐☐☐☐☐

```
m s p a r e s g o l m d
a r m o r s t a r v e e
r r o r e g a r d p r p
t i g a b c r b d e f a
i v m u z z e a f f t r
c h a r m i n g a a c t
l c h r p e q e r v h m
e d d p i h n t e o a e
x o r r m o t t w r r n
w a r e h o u s e a i t
b l l p r e t s l b t p
d n c a r e f u l l y r
s c a r c e l y l e e t
a s h e r i f f e r m t
d e c l a r e t m o t s
```

Spelling Words

spare stare carefully warehouse declare prepare farewell
scarcely various armor article argument starve garbage
charming regard department charity sheriff favorable

VI. Words and Meanings. Write a spelling word for each meaning. Then read down each column to find one spelling word and one **Other Word Form** (p. 75).

a. barely — — — — ☐ — — —

b. aid to the poor — ☐ — — — — —

c. to make ready for a purpose — — — — ☐ — — —

d. consideration or careful thought — — ☐ — — — —

e. a body covering worn in battle — — ☐ — — —

f. a written story on a specific subject — — — ☐ — — —

g. a disagreement — — — — — ☐ — —

h. anything worthless ☐ — — — — — —

i. a good-bye — — — — ☐ — — —

j. to state publicly — — — — ☐ — —

k. cautiously — — ☐ — — — — —

l. extra — — — ☐ —

m. a county's chief law officer — ☐ — — — — —

n. positive or pleasing — — — ☐ — — — —

o. different — — — — — ☐ —

p. to die due to hunger — ☐ — — — —

q. a division or part — ☐ — — — — — —

r. to look long at ☐ — — — —

Write the spelling word and the other word form made by the sets of boxes.

_____ _____

VII. Spinner Words. Spin the letters in each scrambled word to uncover a word in the spelling list. Write the correct word.

a. ardreg _____

b. resta _____

c. ewellfar _____

d. bagegar _____

e. vestar _____

f. orarm _____

g. iousvar _____

h. fsherif _____

i. areprep _____

j. fullycare _____

k. aresp _____

l. mingchar _____

m. houseware _____

n. mentdepart _____

o. itychar _____

p. rablefavo _____

q. clearti _____

r. gumentar _____

s. celyscar _____

t. laredec _____

VIII. All in a Sentence. Use each of the spelling words in sentences about one of the following titles. You may use **Other Word Forms** (p. 75). Circle the spelling words and the other word forms you used.

Stolen Goods or Walking in the Rain

Example: *Walking in the rain is my ⟨favorite⟩ thing to do.*

IX. Final Test. Write each spelling word.

Lesson 20

I. Check Test. Write each spelling word.

II. Spelling Words and Phrases

wealth	lost their **wealth**
healthy	**healthy** sea air
spread	was **spread** on bread
pleasant	was rarely **pleasant**
steady	a **steady** motion
instead	went out **instead**
debt	not deeply in **debt**
depth	unknown **depth**
length	**length** and width
strength	**strength** of an ox
stretch	to bend and **stretch**
wrench	to open with a **wrench**
percent	twenty **percent**
pledge	will **pledge** ten dollars
effort	worth the **effort**
error	corrected my **error**
empire	ancient **empire**
extra	**extra** effort
expert	**expert** advice
expensive	an **expensive** watch

III. Find a Fit. Write each word in its correct shape.

a.
b.
c.
d.
e.
f.
g.
h.
i.
j.
k.
l.
m.
n.
o.
p.
q.
r.
s.
t.

Other Word Forms

wealthy, wealthier, wealthiest, health, healthier, healthiest, spreading, pleasantly, steadies, steadier, steadiest, debts, debtor, depths, lengths, lengthy, strengths, strengthen, strengthened, stretches, stretched, wrenches, wrenched, wrenching, percents, percentage, pledges, pledging, effortless, effortlessly, errors, empires, extras, experts, expertly, expense

IV. Let's Check *E*'s. All the words in the spelling list have a short *e* sound. In alphabetical order, write the spelling words in the correct boxes.

Short *e* Spelled *e*		Short *e* Spelled *ea*
1. _____	8. _____	1. _____
2. _____	9. _____	2. _____
3. _____	10. _____	3. _____
4. _____	11. _____	4. _____
5. _____	12. _____	5. _____
6. _____	13. _____	6. _____
7. _____	14. _____	

V. Likes and Opposites.

a. Write a spelling word for each meaning. Check your answers in the **Glossary/SPELLEX®**.

1. a tool for turning nuts and bolts _____
2. to cover with a thin layer _____
3. additional _____
4. a strong try _____
5. a mistake _____
6. something owed _____
7. a person who has great knowledge on a subject _____
8. to promise _____
9. the parts in each hundred _____
10. as a substitute _____
11. a group of states or nations under one ruler _____
12. the distance from top to bottom _____

b. Write a spelling word for its opposite, or antonym.

1. sickly _____
2. width _____
3. shrink _____
4. shaking _____

5. weakness _____
6. cheap _____
7. disagreeable _____
8. poorness _____

Spelling Words

wealth healthy spread pleasant steady instead debt depth length strength stretch wrench percent pledge effort error empire extra expert expensive

VI. Scrambled Words. Unscramble the underlined words so you can read the signs. Write the unscrambled words.

a. The <u>repimE</u> Supermarket

b. Save up to 40 <u>prentce</u>.

c. Stay <u>thyhale</u>. Use Garble Mouthwash.

d. You can <u>chetstr</u> your food dollar.

e. For that <u>seaplant</u> feeling, use Smeller's Soap!

f. Buy <u>terax</u> food at bargain prices.

g. Avoid the cheaper <u>adespr</u>. Use Butler's Creamy Butter.

h. Buy value <u>nidaest</u> of high costs.

i. Quality and savings is our <u>dgeple</u>.

j. Visit our produce <u>ertpex</u>.

k. We make every <u>rtoffe</u> to serve you well.

l. Special bargains for all our <u>daesty</u> customers.

m. Empire Supermarket only looks <u>spenviexe</u>.

n. Our new computer check-out stations are <u>rerro</u> free.

a. _____

b. _____

c. _____

d. _____

e. _____

f. _____

g. _____

h. _____

i. _____

j. _____

k. _____

l. _____

m. _____

n. _____

VII. Compare and Contrast. Use a spelling word in each of the phrases.

a. not poverty, but _____

b. not profit, but _____

c. not shallowness, but _____

d. not weakness, but _____

e. not a hammer, but a _____

f. not width, but _____

VIII. Writing Headlines. Use each of the spelling words or **Other Word Forms** (p. 79) to write imaginary headlines. Circle the spelling words and the other word forms you used.

Example: *Added (Strength)! New (Wrench) Makes Work (Effortless)*

IX. Final Test. Write each spelling word.

Lesson 21

I. Check Test. Write each spelling word.

II. Spelling Words and Phrases

sting	to **sting** like a bee
stitch	to **stitch** the rip
switch	light **switch**
swiftly	flew away **swiftly**
whisper	a **whisper** in the dark
whistle	a piercing **whistle**
disturb	will **disturb** the silence
acid	an **acid** taste
timid	a **timid** child
rapid	**rapid** transit
stupid	felt very **stupid**
liquid	melted into **liquid**
splendid	**splendid** sunset
forbidden	a **forbidden** place
taxis	**taxis** for hire
campus	college **campus**
wander	to **wander** and wonder
landscape	an icy **landscape**
handkerchief	red **handkerchief**
paragraph	final **paragraph**

III. Find a Fit. Write each word in its correct shape.

a.
b.
c.
d.
e.
f.
g.
h.
i.
j.
k.
l.
m.
n.
o.
p.
q.
r.
s.
t.

Other Word Forms

stinging, stung, stitches, stitched, stitching, switches, switching, swift, swiftest, whispers, whispering, whistled, whistling, disturbing, disturbance, acids, acidic, timidly, rapids, rapidly, stupidly, stupidity, liquids, splendidly, forbid, forbade, forbidding, taxi, campuses, wandered, wanderer, landscapes, handkerchiefs, paragraphs

83

IV. Riddles.

Answer these questions with an <u>id</u> word from the spelling list.

a. What <u>id</u> is not allowed? _____

b. What <u>id</u> is shy? _____

c. What <u>id</u> is wonderful? _____

d. What <u>id</u> burns? _____

e. What <u>id</u> spills? _____

f. What <u>id</u> is not smart? _____

g. What <u>id</u> is fast? _____

Answer these questions with an <u>itch</u> word.

h. What <u>itch</u> is sewn? _____

i. What <u>itch</u> changes? _____

Answer this question with an <u>if</u> word.

j. What <u>if</u> moves quickly? _____

Answer these questions with an <u>is</u> word.

k. What <u>is</u> annoys? _____

l. What <u>is</u> calls a dog? _____

m. What <u>is</u> speaks quietly? _____

n. Sometimes *i* sounds like long *e*.

   What word does this describe? _____

o. Use the six remaining words and as many
   Other Word Forms (p. 83) as you can
   to make a crossword or a word hunt puzzle
   in the grid.

Spelling Words

sting stitch switch swiftly whisper whistle disturb
acid timid rapid stupid liquid splendid forbidden
taxis campus wander landscape handkerchief paragraph

V. Crossword Puzzle. Solve the puzzle by using all the words from the spelling list. Check your answers in the **Glossary/SPELLEX®**.

Across
2. shy
3. to exchange
7. fast
8. to bother
9. college grounds
11. scenery
13. soft speech
14. a small cloth
16. a bee's revenge
18. to sew
19. wonderful

Down
1. a fluid
4. not allowed
5. quickly
6. to travel without a purpose
10. not smart
12. a division of a story
13. a high-pitched, shrill noise
15. a sour, bitter taste
17. cabs

VI. Finding Words.
The words in the spelling list appear in the beginning (A-H), middle (I-Q), or end (R-Z) of the **Glossary/SPELLEX®.** Write each word.

Beginning A-H	Middle I-Q	End R-Z
1. _____	1. _____	1. _____
2. _____	2. _____	2. _____
3. _____	3. _____	3. _____
4. _____		4. _____
5. _____		5. _____
		6. _____
		7. _____
		8. _____
		9. _____
		10. _____
		11. _____
		12. _____

VII. All in a Sentence.
Use each of the spelling words or **Other Word Forms** (p. 83) to write a note to someone you know. Tell about an adventure you had recently. Circle the spelling words and the other word forms you used.

VIII. Final Test.
Write each spelling word.

Lesson 22

I. Check Test. Write each spelling word.

II. Spelling Words and Phrases

loss	profit and **loss**
polish	silver **polish**
volume	great **volume** of water
rotten	a **rotten** banana
project	assigned a **project**
properly	**properly** dressed
gossip	shared some **gossip**
common	**common** cold
comment	to **comment** on it
companion	a loyal **companion**
concert	jazz **concert**
contemplate	will **contemplate** the puzzle
solving	**solving** the mystery
resolve	will **resolve** the problem
response	a friendly **response**
adopt	will **adopt** the child
forehead	sunburned **forehead**
fortune	empty **fortune** cookie
borrowed	**borrowed** a sweater
tailor	made by a **tailor**

III. Find a Fit. Write each word in its correct shape.

a.
b.
c.
d.
e.
f.
g.
h.
i.
j.
k.
l.
m.
n.
o.
p.
q.
r.
s.
t.

Other Word Forms

losses, polishes, polished, polishing, volumes, rot, rottenest, projects, proper, gossips, gossiping, commonly, commented, companions, companionship, concerts, contemplates, contemplating, solve, solved, resolved, resolving, responses, responsible, adopts, adopted, adoption, foreheads, fortunes, fortunately, borrow, borrowing, tailors, tailoring

IV. Sort Your *O*'s. Write each spelling word in the correct box. A word may go in more than one box.

Letter *o* in the First or Only Syllable

1. _____   9. _____
2. _____   10. _____
3. _____   11. _____
4. _____   12. _____
5. _____   13. _____
6. _____   14. _____
7. _____   15. _____
8. _____   16. _____

Letter *o* in the Second Syllable

1. _____   4. _____
2. _____   5. _____
3. _____   6. _____

Letter *o* in the Third Syllable

1. _____

V. Bases and Suffixes. The spelling list contains sixteen base words and four words with suffixes. Write each spelling word.

Words With Suffixes	Base Words	Words With Suffixes	Base Words
a. losses	_____	k. resolved	_____
b. concerts	_____	l. commonly	_____
c. projects	_____	m. contemplates	_____
d. gossiping	_____	n. commented	_____
e. polishing	_____	o. volumes	_____
f. fortunes	_____	p. responses	_____
g. foreheads	_____	q. _____	solve
h. tailoring	_____	r. _____	rot
i. companions	_____	s. _____	borrow
j. adoption	_____	t. _____	proper

Spelling Words

loss polish volume rotten project properly gossip common comment companion concert contemplate solving resolve response adopt forehead fortune borrowed tailor

VI. Synonym Match-ups. Write a spelling word for each synonym.

a. explain _____

b. answer _____

c. remark _____

d. accept _____

e. brow _____

f. rumor _____

g. wealth _____

h. used _____

i. friend _____

j. performance _____

k. decoding _____

l. think _____

m. decayed _____

n. correctly _____

o. ordinary _____

p. shine _____

q. seamstress _____

r. loudness _____

s. assignment _____

t. decrease _____

VII. Building Sentences. Write the following phrases in sentences.

a. a good <u>comment</u>
b. trusted <u>companion</u>
c. <u>properly</u> straightened
d. the fourth <u>volume</u>
e. will <u>polish</u> the ring
f. wrinkled <u>forehead</u>
g. <u>loss</u> of power
h. <u>rotten</u> garbage
i. to <u>adopt</u> an animal
j. outdoor <u>concert</u>
k. <u>solving</u> the puzzle
l. a great <u>fortune</u>
m. <u>common</u> practice
n. to <u>resolve</u> the problem
o. dangerous <u>gossip</u>
p. sewn by a <u>tailor</u>
q. science <u>project</u>
r. correct <u>response</u>
s. to <u>contemplate</u> the matter
t. <u>borrowed</u> a pencil

VIII. Final Test. Write each spelling word.

Lesson 23

I. Check Test. Write each spelling word.

II. Spelling Words and Phrases

bluff	called their **bluff**
cunning	known for its **cunning**
rudder	the boat's **rudder**
suffer	to **suffer** from a fall
succeed	if you can **succeed**
suddenly	**suddenly** fell
suggest	whatever you **suggest**
supply	a **supply** of fresh fruit
support	to **support** the wall
struggle	a **struggle** to breathe
subject	**subject** of a sentence
suspect	to doubt and **suspect**
punctual	always **punctual**
punish	no need to **punish**
publish	will **publish** your story
vulgar	a **vulgar** sight
adjust	to **adjust** the brakes
unjust	an **unjust** decision
result	waited for the **result**
discuss	should **discuss** further

III. Find a Fit. Write each word in its correct shape.

a.
b.
c.
d.
e.
f.
g.
h.
i.
j.
k.
l.
m.
n.
o.
p.
q.
r.
s.
t.

Other Word Forms

bluffs, bluffing, cunningly, rudders, suffered, suffering, succeeded, succeeding, successful, sudden, suggests, suggestion, supplies, supplied, supplying, supported, supportive, struggled, struggling, subjected, subjecting, suspected, suspecting, punctually, punishes, punished, punishment, publishes, publishing, vulgarly, adjusted, just, unjustly, resulted, resulting, discusses, discussion

IV. Hidden Words.
The spelling words can be found in the word puzzle. The words appear across and down. Circle and write the words.

Across

1.
2.
3.
4.
5.
6.
7.
8.

```
s u s p e c t d s u b j e c t
u n u a s u e i u r l s x c r
d j g z u n r s p u u t e n e
d u g w p n p c p d f r p a s
e s e i p i l u o d f u s d u
n t s r l n e s r e m g h j l
l p t n y g r s t r e g d u t
y q p u n i s h p u b l i s h
v u l g a r s r m a q e e t a
p u n c t u a l t p o r s m r
s u f f e r e s u c c e e d o
```

Down

1.
2.
3.
4.
5.
6.
7.
8.
9.
10.
11.
12.

V. Double Your Trouble.
Write the spelling words that fit the patterns below. Each word has a double consonant.

a. blu __ __   _____

b. su __ __ er   _____

c. su __ __ enly   _____

d. ru __ __ er   _____

e. su __ __ eed   _____

f. discu __ __   _____

g. su __ __ est   _____

h. su __ __ ly   _____

i. cu __ __ ing   _____

j. su __ __ ort   _____

k. stru __ __ le   _____

VI. Generally Speaking.
Write a spelling word in the group it best fits.

a. change, fix, _____

b. topic, title, _____

c. ending, conclusion, _____

d. unfair, dishonest, _____

e. on time, early, _____

f. crude, coarse, _____

g. doubt, question, _____

h. discipline, restrict, _____

i. write, print, _____

Spelling Words

bluff cunning rudder suffer succeed suddenly suggest supply support struggle subject suspect punctual punish publish vulgar adjust unjust result discuss

VII. Guide Words. These word pairs are guide words from the **Glossary/SPELLEX®.** Write the words from the spelling list that appear on the same page as each pair of guide words.

abandon—adventure

1. _____

assigned—boil

2. _____

concern—cushion

3. _____

desire—document

4. _____

power—publish

5. _____

punctual—refuse

6. _____
7. _____

regard—scarce

8. _____
9. _____

standard—succeed

10. _____
11. _____
12. _____

sudden—terror

13. _____
14. _____
15. _____
16. _____
17. _____
18. _____

treatment—various

19. _____

vary—wrench

20. _____

VIII. Sentence Detective. Unscramble the word under each blank. Write each unscrambled word.

a. If the _____ of your story will interest many people, the
   bujects

   newspaper will _____ it.
   bupshli

b. The acrobat will _____ his feet to _____ his partner.
   staduj   posrtpu

c. I will _____ you with a ladder so you don't have to
   plyusp

   _____ to wash the windows.
   guelgstr

d. A huge wave _____ smashed against the small boat and tore
   lddensyu

   away its _____ .
   rudedr

e. The judge does _____ the known criminal, but for lack of
   spectus

   evidence she will not _____ him.
   shunip

f. I strongly _____ that you stay away from that
   steggus

   _____ fox.
   ngnunci

g. I will _____ from embarrassment if I am accused of
   ruseff

   _____ behavior.
   guavrl

h. The newscasters will _____ the _____ of the election.
   csdsisu   ltuser

i. The cardplayer's clever _____ will probably _____ .
   fublf   cuecdse

j. The children complained about the _____ punishment for not
   junstu

   being _____ .
   nctluuap

IX. Homographs. Homographs are words that are spelled the same but have different meanings and pronunciations. Use the **Glossary/SPELLEX®** to check the meanings of the homographs below. Then use each homograph in a sentence.

a. sub ject′   b. sub′ ject   c. sus pect′   d. sus′ pect

X. Final Test. Write each spelling word.

94

1	2	3	4	5
acid	effort	instead	spare	suddenly
bluff	extra	properly	splendid	taxis
common	farewell	punctual	strength	timid
contemplate	favorable	rotten	stupid	various
debt	fortune	scarcely	succeed	vulgar

I. Hide and Seek. Twenty-four other word forms and one spelling word can be found in the word puzzle. The words appear across, down, and diagonally. Circle and write each word. If you need help, use the **Glossary/SPELLEX®**.

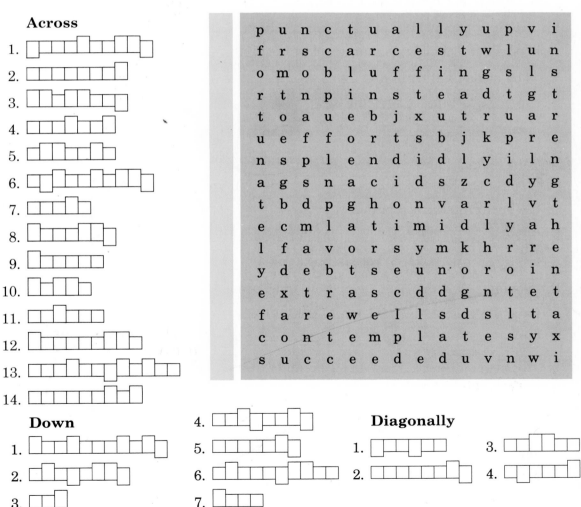

Across

1.
2.
3.
4.
5.
6.
7.
8.
9.
10.
11.
12.
13.
14.

```
p u n c t u a l l y u p v i
f r s c a r c e s t w l u n
o m o b l u f f i n g s l s
r t n p i n s t e a d t g t
t o a u e b j x u t r u a r
u e f f o r t s b j k p r e
n s p l e n d i d l y i l n
a g s n a c i d s z c d y g
t b d p g h o n v a r l v t
e c m l a t i m i d l y a h
l f a v o r s y m k h r r e
y d e b t s e u n o r o i n
e x t r a s c d d g n t e t
f a r e w e l l s d s l t a
c o n t e m p l a t e s y x
s u c c e e d e d u v n w i
```

Down

1.
2.
3.
4.
5.
6.
7.

Diagonally

1.
2.
3.
4.

24

1	2	3	4	5
starve	charity	department	stare	carefully
wealth	spread	percent	error	healthy
whistle	forbidden	liquid	sting	switch
loss	solving	companion	project	struggle
result	unjust	suffer	discuss	response

II. Quotable Quotes. Use other word forms to replace the spelling words printed under the blanks. If you need help, use the **Glossary/SPELLEX**®.

a. "Be _____ not to be _____ ," the beekeeper droned.

carefully ... sting

b. "All of Alice's _____ will be ignored when the _____ is

response ... discuss

over," the hatter chattered madly.

c. "Humpty Dumpty's _____ have _____ in a shattering

error ... result

experience," the king's man cracked openly.

d. "The basketball team has _____ unfortunate _____

suffer ... loss

this season," the coach charged defensively.

e. "Only royal _____ are planned to benefit Snow White's

project

_____ ," the prince contributed charmingly.

charity

f. "Drinking plenty of _____ will improve your _____ ,"

liquid ... healthy

the doctor prescribed patiently.

g. "I've been _____ for half an hour _____ this ginger

struggle ... spread

mixture," the cookie baker snapped crisply.

h. "Some _____ emperors treat people _____ while others

wealth ... unjust

have the golden touch," King Midas reflected radiantly.

i. "_____ these _____ problems," the math teacher added.

solving ... percent

j. "Eight reindeer _____ and I visited hundreds of toy

companion

_____ during December," Santa caroled merrily.

department

k. "I _____ loud _____ ," the coach blasted.

forbidden ... whistle

l. "After _____ at steaks and chops all day, I was _____

stare ... starve

for a hamburger," the broiler cook beefed.

m. "_____ your toothpaste could improve your teeth," the dentist drilled.

switch

96

1	2	3	4	5
armor	declare	regard	sheriff	article
stretch	pledge	expert	empire	length
whisper	landscape	stitch	disturb	wander
volume	resolve	adopt	comment	gossip
adjust	suspect	subject	suggest	publish

III. Word Operations. Use words from the spelling list to complete the exercises. If you need help, use the **Glossary/SPELLEX®**.

a. Operation Past Tense. Write the *ed* form of each word.

1. declare   *declared*   9. pledge _____
2. adjust _____   10. whisper _____
3. armor _____   11. resolve _____
4. adopt _____   12. stitch _____
5. disturb _____   13. gossip _____
6. wander _____   14. comment _____
7. regard _____   15. publish _____
8. stretch _____   16. suggest _____

b. Operation Plural. Write the *s* form of each word.

1. landscape _____   6. empire _____
2. subject _____   7. suspect _____
3. sheriff _____   8. article _____
4. length _____   9. volume _____
5. expert _____

c. Operation Noun. Write the *ion* or *ation* form of each word. Some words need a change before the suffix is added.

1. declare _____   4. suspect _____
2. suggest _____   5. publish _____
3. adopt _____   6. resolve _____

24

1	2	3	4	5
warehouse	garbage	argument	charming	prepare
depth	wrench	steady	expensive	pleasant
rapid	swiftly	handkerchief	campus	paragraph
forehead	tailor	concert	polish	borrowed
support	cunning	supply	punish	rudder

IV. Books and Authors. Use other word forms or the spelling words to fill the blanks in the book titles. Use each word or its other word form only once. Capitalize each word. Use the **Glossary/SPELLEX**®.

a. Beauty and _____ 4 _____ by Izzy Cute

b. Rowing _____ 1 _____ Down the Stream by Whyte Waters

c. Some Rock 'n' Roll _____ 3 _____ by Lowd E. Nuff

d. Reducing Personal _____ 4 _____ by Nita Budgett

e. Eliminating Litter and _____ 2 _____ by Phil D. Dumpster

f. The _____ 2 _____ Foxes by Barry Sligh

g. Backbones and _____ 1 _____ by Ann Atomy

h. Dealing _____ 5 _____ With Others by Willy Smyle Moore

i. The Case of the _____ 4 _____ Apple by T. Churz Pett

j. No More Scolding or _____ 4 _____ by Lett Up

k. Crying Eyes and Dry _____ 3 _____ by Will I. Sobb

l. Cramped Spaces and Filled _____ 1 _____ by Alotta Stock

m. The Student's Guide Book to College _____ 4 _____ by A. Dean

n. New _____ 5 _____ for Old Sailing Ships by Nina N. Pinter

o. Sometimes _____ 3 _____ ; Sometimes Agree by R. B. Trator

p. Screwdrivers and _____ 2 _____ for Every Occasion by Tern N. Twist

q. Writing Better _____ 5 _____ by Letz Wright

r. Safer and _____ 3 _____ Ladders by U. May Clime

s. More a Lender, Less a _____ 5 _____ by Yul B. Richer

t. From the _____ 1 _____ of the Oceans by C. Waters

u. Camping Needs and _____ 3 _____ by Mark A. Trail

v. Be Alert; Be _____ 5 _____ by I. M. Reddy

w. Seamstresses and _____ 2 _____ Through the Ages by Pinz N. Needles

x. Aiding and _____ 1 _____ the Dock Worker by Steve A. Dore

y. Today's Sleekest and _____ 2 _____ Runners by Mara Thonn

Lesson 25

I. Check Test. Write each spelling word.

II. Spelling Words and Phrases

joint	hinge of the **joint**
boiler	steam from the **boiler**
spoil	if the milk will **spoil**
avoid	tried to **avoid**
loyal	**loyal** to friends
voyage	another **voyage**
destroy	accidentally **destroy**
weight	too much **weight**
freight	loaded with **freight**
neighboring	**neighboring** countries
active	an **active** life
action	filled with **action**
athlete	a skillful **athlete**
accent	a southwestern **accent**
patent	should **patent** your invention
pattern	traced the **pattern**
lantern	a flickering **lantern**
salad	soup and **salad**
channel	crossed the **channel**
rapidly	**rapidly** drained out

III. Find a Fit. Write each word in its correct shape.

a.
b.
c.
d.
e.
f.
g.
h.
i.
j.
k.
l.
m.
n.
o.
p.
q.
r.
s.
t.

Other Word Forms

joints, boil, boiled, boiling, spoiled, spoiling, avoids, avoided, avoiding, loyally, loyalty, voyaging, voyager, destroyed, destroying, destruction, weights, weighing, freighter, neighbor, neighbors, actively, activity, actions, athletes, athletic, accents, accenting, patents, patented, patenting, patterns, patterned, lanterns, salads, channels, channeled, rapid

99

IV. Hide and Seek. The spelling words can be found in the word puzzle. The words appear across and down. Circle and write the words.

Across

1.
2.
3.
4.
5.
6.
7.
8.
9.
10.
11.

Down

1.
2.
3.
4.
5.
6.
7.
8.
9.

```
x y z f p a t e n t j h y c
o l b r c g p e a v o i d h
d a w e a c c e n t i b a a
p n e i g h b o r i n g c n
a t i g s p o i l k t l t n
t e g h s s i v t j x w i e
t r h t a p l o y a l n v l
e n t e l i e u a y z m e k
r f b h a l r a p i d l y n
n i d c d a c t i o n m o l
g a t h l e t e v o y a g e
j d e s t r o y p t o r q u
```

V. Word Match-ups. Write a spelling word that best fits each phrase or word below.

a. goods _____

b. travel _____

c. dodge _____

d. to wreck _____

e. quickly _____

f. lamp _____

g. next to _____

h. busy _____

i. faithful _____

j. rot _____

k. model used for tracing _____

l. one who takes part in sports _____

m. mixture of vegetables _____

n. knee or elbow _____

o. a hot-water storage tank _____

p. heaviness _____

q. sole rights for an invention _____

r. TV station _____

s. local speech pattern _____

t. movement _____

Spelling Words

joint boiler spoil avoid loyal voyage destroy weight freight neighboring active action athlete accent patent pattern lantern salad channel rapidly

VI. Finding Words. The words in the spelling list appear in the beginning (A-H), middle (I-Q), or end (R-Z) of the **Glossary/SPELLEX®**. Write each word.

Beginning A-H		Middle I-Q	End R-Z
1. _____	5. _____	1. _____	1. _____
2. _____	6. _____	2. _____	2. _____
3. _____	7. _____	3. _____	3. _____
4. _____	8. _____	4. _____	4. _____
	9. _____	5. _____	5. _____
		6. _____	

VII. The Treasure Map. Unscramble the scrambled words to form words from the spelling list.

a. teparnt __ __ ☐ __ __ __ __

b. eghtifr __ __ __ __ ☐ __

c. cantec __ __ __ ☐ __ __

d. trnanel __ __ __ __ ☐ __ __

e. strodey __ __ __ __ __ ☐ __

f. laloy __ __ ☐ __ __

g. intoca ☐ __ __ __ __ __

h. dlsaa __ __ ☐ __ __

i. intjo ☐ __ __ __ __

j. agyvoe __ __ __ __ __ ☐

k. ewight ☐ __ __ __ __ __

l. thelate __ __ __ __ __ ☐ __

m. lennach __ __ __ __ __ __ ☐

n. spoli ☐ __ __ __ __

Write the boxed letter in each spelling word in order (a-n), and find out what is in the treasure chest: __ __ __   __ __ __ __ __ __   __ __ __ __ __ .

101

VIII. Writing Sentences. Write each set of words in a sentence. You may use **Other Word Forms** (p. 99).

1. action—patent—pattern

2. salad—weight—avoid

3. boiler—destroy—active

4. athlete—rapidly—joint

5. channel—neighboring—voyage

6. freight—lantern—spoil

7. loyal—accent

IX. Final Test. Write each spelling word.

Lesson 26

I. Check Test. Write each spelling word.

II. Spelling Words and Phrases

metal	new **metal** detector
method	standard **method**
gentle	in a **gentle** way
velvet	a **velvet** cushion
lettuce	head of **lettuce**
seldom	**seldom** smiled
selfish	a **selfish** reason
special	for a **special** day
whether	**whether** to go
accept	to **accept** first prize
affect	will **affect** your plans
collect	to **collect** a pailful
expect	can **expect** a crowd
respect	a sign of **respect**
neglect	care or **neglect**
object	if they **object**
insects	as **insects** fly by
directed	used as **directed**
defense	the country's **defense**
expense	much greater **expense**

III. Find a Fit. Write each word in its correct shape.

a.
b.
c.
d.
e.
f.
g.
h.
i.
j.
k.
l.
m.
n.
o.
p.
q.
r.
s.
t.

Other Word Forms

metals, metallic, methods, gently, gentler, gentlest, velvety, selfishly, specials, specialize, specialty, accepts, accepting, affected, affecting, collected, collecting, collection, expected, expecting, respected, respectable, neglected, neglectful, objected, objecting, objection, insect, direct, directing, direction, defend, defending, defender, defensive, expensive

IV. Word Riddles. Answer each question with an <u>ect</u>, <u>ense</u>, <u>sel</u>, or <u>met</u> word from the spelling list.

a. What <u>ect</u> do you give to elders? _____

b. What <u>ect</u> makes you sad? _____

c. What <u>ect</u> influences or changes? _____

d. What <u>ect</u> opposes something? _____

e. What <u>ect</u> can bug you? _____

f. What <u>ect</u> might you do with stamps? _____

g. What <u>ect</u> do you await? _____

h. What <u>ect</u> did the band leader do? _____

i. What <u>ense</u> is provided by a fort? _____

j. What <u>ense</u> stops you from buying? _____

k. What <u>sel</u> tells how often Valentine's Day comes? _____

l. What <u>sel</u> describes a stingy person? _____

m. What <u>met</u> shines when polished? _____

n. What <u>met</u> is a way of doing something? _____

Write the six remaining spelling words in alphabetical order.

1. _____   4. _____

2. _____   5. _____

3. _____   6. _____

Spelling Words

metal   method   gentle   velvet   lettuce   seldom   selfish
special   whether   accept   affect   collect   expect   respect   neglect
object   insects   directed   defense   expense

V. Hide and Seek. The spelling words can be found in the word puzzle. The words appear across, down, and diagonally. Circle and write the words.

Across

1.
2.
3.
4.
5.
6.

Down

1.
2.
3.
4.
5.
6.
7.
8.
9.
10.

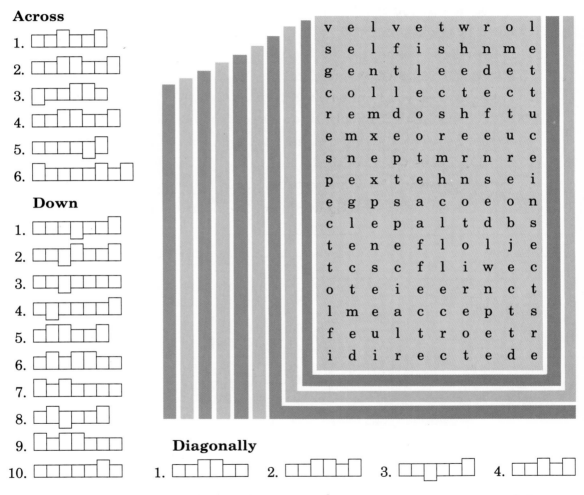

Diagonally

1.   2.   3.   4.

VI. Homographs. Use the **Glossary/SPELLEX®** to check the meanings of the homographs below. Then use each homograph in a sentence.

a. ob ject'   b. ob' ject   c. af fect'   d. af' fect

VII. Writing Short Stories. Use all of the spelling words or **Other Word Forms** (p. 103) to write two short stories with the following titles. Use each spelling word only once between the two stories. Circle the spelling words and the other word forms you used.

Through the Frightening Jungle

Yesterday's Homework

VIII. Final Test. Write each spelling word.

Lesson 27

I. Check Test. Write each spelling word.

II. Spelling Words and Phrases

abandon	had to **abandon** ship
advantage	took **advantage** of
advertise	will **advertise** on TV
accident	to witness the **accident**
attractive	an **attractive** family
battery	a flashlight **battery**
passage	had read a short **passage**
traffic	as **traffic** thinned
happiness	shared our **happiness**
cabinet	from the **cabinet**
capital	a **capital** letter
catalog	1400-page **catalog**
chapter	the last **chapter**
vanity	pride and **vanity**
practical	a **practical** set of tools
factories	shoe **factories**
exactly	**exactly** on time
example	a good **example**
traveler	a tired **traveler**
material	stronger **material**

III. Find a Fit. Write each word in its correct shape.

a.
b.
c.
d.
e.
f.
g.
h.
i.
j.
k.
l.
m.
n.
o.
p.
q.
r.
s.
t.

Other Word Forms

abandons, abandoned, abandoning, advantages, advertises, advertised, advertising, advertisement, accidents, accidentally, attract, attractively, batteries, passages, passenger, happy, happiest, cabinets, capitals, catalogs, chapters, vain, vanities, practice, practically, factory, exact, exactness, examples, travel, traveled, traveling, travelers, materials, materialize

IV. Generally Speaking. Write each spelling word in the group it best fits. Next to all but one spelling word, write an **Other Word Form** (p. 107).

Other Word Forms

a. accurately, carefully, _____   _____

b. book division, several passages, _____   _____

c. pretty, appealing, _____   _____

d. main city, Washington, D.C., _____   _____

e. power, dry cell, _____   _____

f. order form, book, _____   _____

g. pride, boastfulness, _____   _____

h. sample, model, _____   _____

i. cloth, fabric, _____   _____

j. leave, desert, _____   _____

k. crash, dent, _____   _____

l. joy, pleasure, _____   _____

m. sensible, useful, _____   _____

n. cupboard, closet, _____   _____

o. head start, benefit, _____   _____

p. sell, announce, _____   _____

q. buildings, industries, _____   _____

r. tourist, hiker, _____   _____

s. section, paragraph, _____   _____

t. vehicles, noise, _____

Spelling Words

abandon advantage advertise accident attractive battery passage traffic happiness cabinet capital catalog chapter vanity material practical factories exactly example traveler

V. Story Scramble. Unscramble each underlined word in the story. Then write the unscrambled words. One word will be an **Other Word Form** (p. 107).*

The Auto Search

During my early search for a car, I checked every (a.) goalcat to find the most (b.) lacticapr yet (c.) vittactare car (d.) vaderdiets.* Since my (e.) palatic was limited, I first had to (f.) bandona my dream of a luxury car. Taking (g.) actlexy five thousand dollars that I had carefully tucked away in the kitchen (h.) bactine, I visited several dealerships. I took (i.) gatenavad of any offer to go on a test drive. During one test drive in heavy (j.) fatrfic, where (k.) ssgeapa was difficult, I had an (l.) ccaintde. The cables were jarred from the (m.) tertaby, and a tow truck had to be called to make other repairs. Finally, after countless test drives, I found the car that brought me (n.) spipahnes. The leather (o.) liartame used for the upholstery was one of the many fine features that sold me on this car.

Now I am a frequent (p.) vearletr who sells machine parts to several (q.) seorifact throughout the state. I even have (r.) nivaty plates. This long search was truly an (s.) mpxeael of determination! Thus ends the final (t.) preacht of my story.

a. _____   h. _____   o. _____

b. _____   i. _____   p. _____

c. _____   j. _____   q. _____

d. _____   k. _____   r. _____

e. _____   l. _____   s. _____

f. _____   m. _____   t. _____

g. _____   n. _____

VI. Base Words.
The spelling list contains thirteen base words and seven words that are not base words. Write each spelling word.

Words That Are Not Base Words	Base Words	Words That Are Not Base Words	Base Words
a. accidentally	_____	k. advantages	_____
b. advertisement	_____	l. passages	_____
c. capitals	_____	m. _____	happy
d. abandoning	_____	n. _____	vain
e. examples	_____	o. _____	practice
f. materials	_____	p. _____	factory
g. batteries	_____	q. _____	exact
h. cabinets	_____	r. _____	attract
i. catalogs	_____	s. _____	travel
j. chapters	_____		

Write the one base word not used above. _____

VII. All in a Sentence.
Write each of the spelling words in sentences about one of the following titles. You may use **Other Word Forms** (p. 107). Circle the spelling words and the other word forms you used.

The Election or A Department Store

Example: *There is a department store located in an old* (factory) .

VIII. Final Test.
Write each spelling word.

Lesson 28

I. Check Test. Write each spelling word.

II. Spelling Words and Phrases

limit	to **limit** their time
spirit	played with **spirit**
admit	to **admit** we're wrong
credit	to their **credit**
profit	will **profit** greatly
exhibit	a crafts **exhibit**
deposit	made a bank **deposit**
permitted	no animals **permitted**
permission	**permission** to leave
twist	to **twist** out of shape
assist	can **assist** me later
insist	if you **insist**
dentist	went to the **dentist**
impulse	a sudden **impulse**
inning	may win in the final **inning**
income	earned a good **income**
dismiss	to **dismiss** for recess
district	school **district**
slippers	tripped over **slippers**
scissors	to cut with **scissors**

III. Find a Fit. Write each word in its correct shape.

a.
b.
c.
d.
e.
f.
g.
h.
i.
j.
k.
l.
m.
n.
o.
p.
q.
r.
s.
t.

Other Word Forms

limited, limiting, limitation, spirited, admitted, admitting, admittance, credits, credited, crediting, profited, profiting, exhibited, exhibition, deposited, depositing, permit, permitting, twisted, twisting, assisted, assistant, insisted, insisting, dentists, dentistry, impulses, innings, incomes, incoming, dismisses, dismissing, dismissal, districts, slip, slipper, slippery

IV. The _I_'s Have It. All the spelling words have a short _i_ sound. Write each spelling word in the correct box. A word may go in more than one box.

Words That End With _it_

1. _____
2. _____
3. _____
4. _____
5. _____
6. _____
7. _____

Words That End With _ist_

1. _____
2. _____
3. _____
4. _____

Words With a Short _i_ Sound Followed by a Double Consonant

1. _____
2. _____
3. _____
4. _____
5. _____
6. _____

Words With _i_ in Two Syllables

1. _____
2. _____
3. _____
4. _____
5. _____
6. _____
7. _____
8. _____

The Two Words That Did Not Fit in Any Other Box

1. _____
2. _____

V. Generally Speaking. Write each of the spelling words in the group it best fits.

a. area, section, _____

b. put in, place, _____

c. doctor, teeth, _____

d. feeling, urge, _____

e. salary, pay, _____

f. turn, bend, _____

g. aid, help, _____

h. end, boundary, _____

i. cutters, shears, _____

j. shoes, sandals, _____

k. pay later, charge, _____

l. playing time, round, _____

m. excuse, send away, _____

n. approved, allowed, _____

o. show, display, _____

p. allow in, accept as true, _____

q. demand, declare, _____

r. increase, gain, _____

s. liveliness, enthusiasm, _____

t. OK, consent, _____

112

Spelling Words

limit spirit admit credit profit exhibit deposit
permitted permission twist assist insist dentist impulse
inning income dismiss district slippers scissors

VI. Guide Words. These word pairs are guide words from the **Glossary/SPELLEX®**. Write the words from the spelling list that appear on the same page as each pair of guide words.

abandon—adventure

1. _____

assigned—boil

2. _____

concern—cushion

3. _____

customer—design

4. _____

5. _____

desire—document

6. _____

7. _____

evil—fault

8. _____

hesitate—insect

9. _____

10. _____

11. _____

insects—knowledge

12. _____

labor—machine

13. _____

perform—poultry

14. _____

15. _____

power—publish

16. _____

scarcely—sicken

17. _____

silent—staff

18. _____

19. _____

treatment—various

20. _____

VII. Where Is *It*? Spin each scrambled *it* word to get a word from the spelling list. Then write each word in a question.

a. itlim   _____

b. itcred   _____

c. itspir   _____

d. itprof   _____

e. itadm   _____

f. itdepos   _____

g. itexhib   _____

h. ittedperm   _____

VIII. What *Is* Is Missing? Putting *is* between the correct letters, write a word from the spelling list. Then write each word or its **Other Word Form** (p. 111) in a command.

a. asst   _____

b. dentt   _____

c. scsors   _____

d. permsion   _____

e. dtrict   _____

f. twt   _____

g. inst   _____

h. disms   _____

IX. Word Parts. Add ending word parts from the box to complete four spelling words. Write the words.

pulse	pers	ing	come

a. in + _____ = _____

b. im + _____ = _____

c. inn + _____ = _____

d. slip + _____ = _____

X. Final Test. Write each spelling word.

I. Check Test. Write each spelling word.

II. Spelling Words and Phrases

customer	one to a **customer**
runaway	**runaway** horse
submarine	an atomic **submarine**
republic	flag of the **republic**
instruction	swimming **instruction**
difficult	**difficult** to refuse
stomach	**stomach** trouble
onion	strong **onion** smell
countries	neighboring **countries**
suitable	**suitable** for framing
firm	a **firm** handshake
thirsty	**thirsty** hikers
Thursday	to deliver on **Thursday**
purple	a **purple** grape
burden	a heavy **burden**
curtain	closed the **curtain**
furniture	outdoor **furniture**
courage	known for **courage**
government	**government** offices
otherwise	will leave **otherwise**

III. Find a Fit. Write each word in its correct shape.

a.
b.
c.
d.
e.
f.
g.
h.
i.
j.
k.
l.
m.
n.
o.
p.
q.
r.
s.
t.

Other Word Forms

customers, runaways, submarines, republics, instruct, instructs, instructor, instructions, difficulty, difficulties, stomachs, onions, country, suit, suitably, firmest, firmly, thirst, thirstily, Thurs., purpled, purplish, burdens, curtains, furnish, courageous, govern, governs, governing, governor, governments

IV. All in a Row.
Write the twenty spelling words in alphabetical order. Then join the boxed letters and write four hidden words.

1. __ ☐ __ __ __ __
2. __ __ ☐ __ __ __ __ ☐
3. __ __ ☐ __ __ __
4. __ __ ☐ __ __
5. __ __ __ __ __ ☐ __

Hidden Word: _____

6. ☐ __ __ __ ☐ __ __ __ __
7. ☐ __ __ __
8. ☐ __ __ __ __ __ __
9. __ __ __ ☐ __ __ __ __ __
10. __ __ __ __ ☐ __ __ __ __ __ __

Hidden Word: _____

11. __ __ __ __ ☐
12. __ __ __ __ __ __ ☐ __ __
13. __ __ __ ☐ __ __ __ __
14. __ __ ☐ __ __ __ __ __
15. __ __ __ __ __ __ ☐

Hidden Word: _____

16. __ ☐ __ __ __ __ __
17. __ __ __ __ ☐ __ ☐ __ ☐
18. __ __ __ __ ☐ __ __ __
19. __ __ __ __ ☐ __ __
20. __ __ __ __ __ __ ☐

Hidden Word: _____

V. Base Words.
The spelling list contains fourteen base words and six words that are not base words. Write each spelling word.

Words That Are Not Base Words	Base Words	Words That Are Not Base Words	Base Words
a. firmly	_____	j. difficulty	_____
b. curtains	_____	k. republics	_____
c. submarines	_____	l. runaways	_____
d. onions	_____	m. _____ thirst	
e. courageous	_____	n. _____ instruct	
f. customers	_____	o. _____ suit	
g. purpled	_____	p. _____ country	
h. stomachs	_____	q. _____ govern	
i. burdens	_____	r. _____ furnish	

Write the two base words not used above. _____ _____

Spelling Words

customer runaway submarine republic instruction difficult stomach onion countries suitable firm thirsty Thursday purple burden curtain furniture courage government otherwise

VI. Crossword Puzzle. Solve the puzzle by using all the words from the spelling list. One word will be an **Other Word Form** (p. 115).* Check your answers in the **Glossary/SPELLEX®**.

Across

1. France and Spain
3. an underwater vessel
5. tables and chairs
7. a vegetable
8. a country's system of rules
13. a day of the week
14. a dark color
15. one who makes a purchase
16. hard to do
17. a window covering
18. proper or fitting

Down

1. bravery
2. differently
4. out of control
5. unshaking; steady
6. lessons*
9. the organ that digests food
10. needing water
11. a type of government
12. a load

117

VII. Writing Sentences. Write each set of words in a sentence. You may use **Other Word Forms** (p. 115).

1. republic—countries—government

2. submarine—runaway—courage

3. otherwise—suitable—customer

4. difficult—instruction—burden

5. onion—stomach—thirsty

6. purple—furniture—curtain

7. firm—Thursday

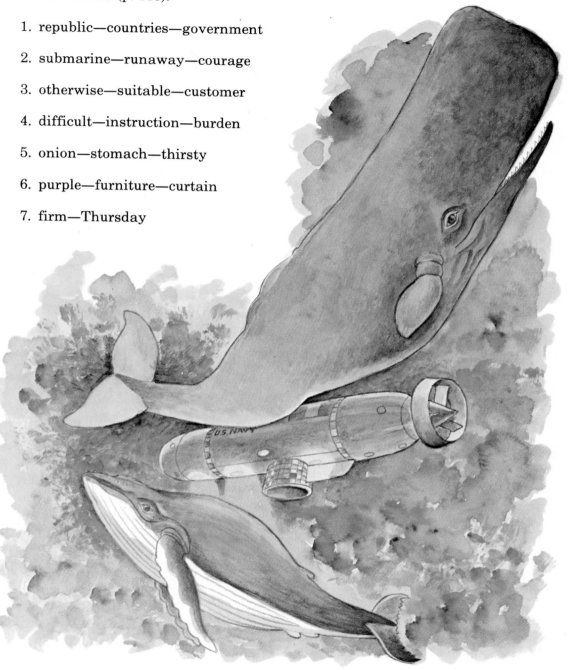

VIII. Final Test. Write each spelling word.

1	2	3	4	5
freight	collect	cabinet	spirit	Thursday
voyage	special	vanity	slippers	onion
channel	expense	catalog	dentist	thirsty
weight	insects	factories	admit	purple
lantern	gentle	material	scissors	stomach

I. Sentences in Paragraphs. Write other word forms or the spelling words to complete the sentences. Use the words from column 1 to complete paragraph 1, and so on. Write each word or its other word form only once. If you need help, use the **Glossary/SPELLEX®.**

1.   A _____ is a large ship that makes _____ through waterways known as _____ . Every piece of cargo is _____ before being placed on board. Unlike ships long ago, freighters use electricity, not gas _____ .

2.   Some people enjoy _____ rocks, stamps, and coins. There are shops which _____ in selling different collectors' items. Buying these items can be very _____ . I know of a person who purchased an addition for his _____ collection. He handles this insect very _____ , since it is his most expensive purchase.

3.   My cousins have a talent for carpentry work. Recently, they built new kitchen _____ for my aunt. My cousins are not boastful or _____ about their work. Sometimes they look through _____ for ideas. They plan to visit a cabinet _____ soon so they can see how different wood _____ are used.

4.   With very low _____ , I usually _____ quietly into any _____ office. I have always _____ that I have a fear of sharp objects such as knives, _____ , and drills!

5.   On _____ the cooks served sandwiches with _____ for lunch. Within one hour we all had a _____ for water. Several students began turning a _____ color in history class and complained that their _____ were upset.

119

30

1	2	3	4	5
active	capital	expect	instruction	passage
affect	deposit	firm	joint	permission
assist	destroy	government	limit	respect
attractive	difficult	happiness	neglect	selfish
avoid	example	impulse	neighboring	suitable

II. Before and After. Find the spelling word that comes alphabetically right *before* each word below. Write the spelling word and an other word form for each spelling word. If you need help, use the **Glossary/SPELLEX®**.

Before	**Spelling Words**	**Other Word Forms**
a. neither	n e i g h b o r i n g	*neighbors*
b. neighbor	— — — — — —	
c. linen	— — — — —	
d. exchange	— — — — — — —	
e. patent	— — — — — —	
f. senior	— — — — — — —	
g. awful	— — — — —	
h. flavor	— — — —	
i. direct	— — — — — — — — —	
j. journey	— — — — —	
k. insure	— — — — — — — — —	
l. happy	— — — — — — — — —	

Now find the spelling word that comes alphabetically right *after* each word below. Write the spelling word and an other word form for each spelling word.

After	**Spelling Words**	**Other Word Forms**
m. action	a c t i v e	
n. dessert	— — — — — — —	
o. resort	— — — — — — —	
p. improvement	— — — — — — —	
q. govern	— — — — — — — — — —	
r. suit	— — — — — — — —	
s. advise	— — — — — —	
t. department	— — — — — — —	
u. attract	— — — — — — — — — —	
v. capable	— — — — — — —	
w. assigned	— — — — — —	
x. permanent	— — — — — — — — — —	
y. exhibit	— — — — — —	

1	2	3	4	5
salad	traveler	accept	boiler	accent
pattern	object	directed	method	velvet
abandon	battery	chapter	advertise	exhibit
submarine	twist	dismiss	permitted	curtain
credit	furniture	otherwise	customer	rapidly

III. Classified Ads. Complete each ad by writing other word forms or the spelling words. The number tells you in what column you can find the spelling word. Use each word or its other word form only once. If you need help, use the **Glossary/SPELLEX®**.

a. Restaurant ad: No soggy green (1) _____ served.

b. Clothes designer ad: We pin (1) _____ perfectly.

c. Furnace repair shop ad: We're hot on mending (4) _____ .

d. Language teacher ad: All (5) _____ accepted.

e. Boat captain ad: We (2) _____ in waves.

f. Secondhand store ad: Our business is (3) _____ your rejects.

g. Dime store ad: Odd (2) _____ are our specialty.

h. Barbershop ad: Two new (4) _____ to end baldness.

i. Filmmaker ad: A (3) _____ needed for reel-life drama.

j. Airline ad: Soft (5) _____ seats make for soft landings.

k. Book writer ad: Ten (3) _____ in ten days.

l. Zookeeper ad: Caretakers wanted for (1) _____ anteaters.

m. Bus tour ad: As (4) _____ , discount rates start this week.

n. Gas station ad: We charge (2) _____ for free.

o. Computer company ad: Visit both (5) _____ ; we need your input.

p. School ad: Enroll at our school; daily (3) _____ guaranteed.

q. Pasta maker ad: We teach spaghetti (2) _____ to teens.

r. Sailor ad: Need water for (1) _____ ; (3) _____ we walk.

s. State park ad: Picnicking (4) _____ required.

t. Mirror and glass store ad: Our best (4) _____ are window shoppers.

u. Cabinet maker ad: Fancy (2) _____ made while you wait.

v. Window store ad: Corduroy (5) _____ come pleated.

w. Track team ad: Very (5) _____ runners required.

x. Discount store ad: Your (1) _____ is good but your cash is better.

30

1	2	3	4	5
traffic	accident	courage	lettuce	defense
seldom	profit	inning	republic	practical
countries	loyal	patent	advantage	runaway
spoil	metal	exactly	athlete	action
insist	burden	whether	district	income

IV. Words in a Series. Use other word forms or the spelling words to complete each series. The number tells you in what column you can find the spelling word. Use each word or its other word form only once.

a. greens, cabbage, (4) _____

b. cars, buses, (1) _____

c. governments, democracies, (4) _____

d. unplanned, unintended, (2) _____

e. bravery, fearlessness, (3) _____

f. powerless, helpless, (5) _____

g. actually, sensibly, (5) _____

h. rarely, hardly, (1) _____

i. region, state, (1) _____

j. gains, rewards, (2) _____

k. periods, quarters, (3) _____

l. invented, created, (3) _____

m. trueness, faithfulness, (2) _____

n. correct, right, (3) _____

o. benefits, gains, (4) _____

p. stowaways, stampeding animals, (5) _____

q. decayed, rotten, (1) _____

r. ores, minerals, (2) _____

s. ballplayers, swimmers, (4) _____

t. movements, deeds, (5) _____

u. earnings, salaries, (5) _____

v. areas, sections, (4) _____

w. weights, loads, (2) _____

x. demands, requires, (1) _____

y. either, if, (3) _____

Lesson 31

I. Check Test. Write each spelling word.

II. Spelling Words and Phrases

enemies	friends or **enemies**
envelope	a stamped **envelope**
elevator	**elevator** to the lobby
exercise	an **exercise** bicycle
express	shipped by **express**
extent	the **extent** of the trouble
prevent	to **prevent** the theft
cement	**cement** wall
element	an important **element**
settlement	to build a **settlement**
independent	an **independent** person
represent	will **represent** the owner
presented	**presented** an award
memory	lost my **memory**
membership	**membership** in a club
century	turn of the **century**
several	**several** oval shapes
skeleton	**skeleton** bones
reckless	needlessly **reckless**
arrest	under **arrest**

III. Find a Fit. Write each word in its correct shape.

a.
b.
c.
d.
e.
f.
g.
h.
i.
j.
k.
l.
m.
n.
o.
p.
q.
r.
s.
t.

Other Word Forms

enemy, envelopes, elevate, elevating, exercises, exercising, expresses, expressing, expression, extend, extents, extension, prevented, preventative, prevention, cemented, cementing, elements, settle, settling, independently, representing, representative, representation, present, presenting, presentation, memories, member, memberships, centuries, skeletons, recklessly, arrests, arresting

IV. Sort Your *E*'s. Each word in the spelling list has at least one *e*. Write each word in the correct box.

One *e*

1. _____   2. _____   3. _____

Two *e*'s

1. _____   4. _____   7. _____
2. _____   5. _____   8. _____
3. _____   6. _____   9. _____

Three *e*'s

1. _____   4. _____   7. _____
2. _____   5. _____   8. _____
3. _____   6. _____

V. Bases and Suffixes. The spelling list contains fifteen base words and five words with suffixes. Write each spelling word.

Words With Suffixes	Base Words	Words With Suffixes	Base Words
a. extents	_____	k. exercises	_____
b. skeletons	_____	l. elements	_____
c. cementing	_____	m. recklessly	_____
d. representative	_____	n. centuries	_____
e. expressing	_____	o. _____	present
f. prevention	_____	p. _____	settle
g. envelopes	_____	q. _____	elevate
h. memories	_____	r. _____	enemy
i. independently	_____	s. _____	member
j. arresting	_____		

Write the one base word not used above. _____

Spelling Words

enemies envelope elevator exercise express extent prevent
cement element settlement independent represent presented
memory membership century several skeleton reckless arrest

VI. What's the Suggestion? Write a word from the spelling list for each suggestion.

a. One word suggests bones: _____

b. One word suggests dues: _____

c. One word suggests police officer: _____

d. One word suggests a daredevil: _____

e. One word suggests a hundred: _____

f. One word suggests push-ups: _____

g. One word suggests a chemical substance: _____

h. One word suggests postage: _____

i. One word suggests remembering: _____

j. One word suggests a colony: _____

k. One word suggests alone: _____

l. One word suggests glue: _____

m. One word suggests a rapid train: _____

n. One word suggests up and down: _____

o. One word suggests some: _____

p. One word suggests given: _____

q. One word suggests a lawyer: _____

r. One word suggests stopping: _____

s. One word suggests distance: _____

t. One word suggests hateful people: _____

VII. Writing Headlines. Use each of the spelling words or an **Other Word Form** (p. 123) to write some imaginary headlines. Circle the spelling words and the other word forms you used.

Example: (*Envelope*) *Containing* (*Several*) *Hundred Dollars Found*

VIII. Final Test. Write each spelling word.

Lesson 32

I. Check Test. Write each spelling word.

II. Spelling Words and Phrases

strict	**strict** but fair
stingy	selfish and **stingy**
pity	filled with **pity**
simply	**simply** made
misery	**misery** and fever
mineral	**mineral** water
citizen	Canadian **citizen**
prisoner	**prisoner** of war
victory	the glory of **victory**
dictionary	heavy **dictionary**
division	long **division**
provisions	carried **provisions**
admission	paid **admission**
ability	**ability** to win
activity	sports **activity**
delivery	**delivery** truck
continue	will **continue** the work
submit	to **submit** a report
impossible	**impossible** mission
business	electronics **business**

III. Find a Fit. Write each word in its correct shape.

a.
b.
c.
d.
e.
f.
g.
h.
i.
j.
k.
l.
m.
n.
o.
p.
q.
r.
s.
t.

Other Word Forms

strictly, stingier, stingiest, pities, pitying, pitiful, simple, simplest, simplicity, miseries, miserable, minerals, citizenship, prison, victories, victorious, dictionaries, divide, dividing, provide, provided, providing, admit, admitting, admittance, abilities, active, activities, delivering, deliveries, continues, continued, continuous, submitted, possible, impossibly, impossibility, busy, businesses

IV. Sort Your Vowels. Write each spelling word in the correct box.

a. Write all the words with a long *e* sound spelled *y*.

1. _____   4. _____   7. _____

2. _____   5. _____   8. _____

3. _____   6. _____   9. _____

b. Write all the words *not* used above with two or more *i*'s.

1. _____   3. _____   5. _____

2. _____   4. _____

c. Write the remaining words with a short *i* sound.

1. _____   3. _____   5. _____

2. _____   4. _____   6. _____

V. Guide Words. These word pairs are guide words from the **Glossary/SPELLEX®**. Write the words from the spelling list that appear on the same page as each pair of guide words.

abandon—adventure

1. _____

2. _____

3. _____

boiler—chalk

4. _____

chamber—computer

5. _____

concern—cushion

6. _____

customer—design

7. _____

desire—document

8. _____

9. _____

hesitate—insect

10. _____

machinery—mining

11. _____

minor—nowhere

12. _____

perform—poultry

13. _____

power—publish

14. _____

15. _____

silent—staff

16. _____

standard—succeed

17. _____

18. _____

19. _____

vary—wrench

20. _____

Spelling Words

*strict stingy pity simply misery mineral citizen
prisoner victory dictionary division provisions admission
ability activity delivery continue submit impossible business*

VI. Generally Speaking. Write the spelling word that best fits each group or phrase below.

a. company, store, _____

b. alphabetical word book, _____

c. go on, proceed, _____

d. separation, section, _____

e. entrance fee, price, _____

f. native, resident, _____

g. ungenerous, scanty, _____

h. captive, convict, _____

i. hopeless, unthinkable, _____

j. project, game, _____

k. talent, skill, _____

l. easily, plainly, _____

m. suffering, unhappiness, _____

n. win, success, _____

o. metal, ore, _____

p. package, distribution, _____

q. sorrow, sympathy, _____

r. food, supplies, _____

s. stern, firm, _____

t. surrender, give up, _____

VII. Hidden Words. Read each sentence to find clues to the hidden spelling words. Circle the word hidden in each set of underlined words. Write each word.

a. The <u>miner</u> <u>allowed</u> me to check the ore.   _____

b. The <u>victor</u> <u>yearned</u> to claim her prize.   _____

c. The <u>prison</u> <u>erupted</u> with shouts from the convict.   _____

d. Your <u>remarks</u> <u>imply</u> that the work is not complicated.   _____

e. The meat company did <u>provide</u> <u>liver</u> <u>yesterday</u> to the customers' homes.   _____

VIII. Book List. Using all of the spelling words, make up titles for books. You may use **Other Word Forms** (p. 127). Circle the spelling words and the other word forms you used.

Example: *The* (*Victorious*) (*Citizen*)

IX. Final Test. Write each spelling word.

Lesson 33

I. Check Test. Write each spelling word.

II. Spelling Words and Phrases

author	a wordy **author**
auction	used-car **auction**
caution	will enter with **caution**
fault	your **fault**
pause	to **pause** to breathe
launch	to **launch** a rocket
laundry	dirty **laundry**
thoughtful	looking **thoughtful**
chalk	eraser and **chalk**
awfully	**awfully** upset
awkward	an **awkward** move
lawyers	books for **lawyers**
opera	**opera** singer
colonies	**colonies** of insects
positive	**positive** or negative
opposite	not **opposite** but similar
knowledge	scientific **knowledge**
astonished	**astonished** by the news
squash	**squash** on the vine
vacant	a **vacant** lot

III. Find a Fit. Write each word in its correct shape.

a.
b.
c.
d.
e.
f.
g.
h.
i.
j.
k.
l.
m.
n.
o.
p.
q.
r.
s.
t.

Other Word Forms

authors, auctions, auctioned, auctioneer, cautioning, cautious, faults, faulty, pauses, paused, pausing, launches, launched, launching, laundries, think, thinking, thought, chalky, awful, awkwardly, lawyer, operas, colony, colonist, colonize, positively, oppose, opposites, knowledgeable, astonish, astonishes, astonishing, astonishment, squashes, squashed, vacate, vacating, vacancy, vacantly

IV. Across and Down.
The spelling words can be found in the word puzzle. The words appear across and down. Circle and write the words.

Across

1.
2.
3.
4.
5.
6.
7.
8.
9.
10.
11.
12.

```
l  p  m  f  o  n  a  l  a  w  y  e  r  s  r
s  q  u  a  s  h  s  c  o  p  i  n  y  o  n
j  u  k  u  r  s  t  l  a  u  n  c  h  p  y
i  h  v  l  t  u  o  p  p  o  s  i  t  e  k
a  u  c  t  i  o  n  c  h  a  l  k  b  r  n
g  w  c  a  u  t  i  o  n  q  u  a  c  a  o
a  a  f  b  c  d  s  r  a  p  a  u  s  e  w
w  w  v  w  u  t  h  o  u  g  h  t  f  u  l
k  f  a  a  l  t  e  t  t  j  f  h  k  d  e
w  u  c  l  q  u  d  d  h  i  g  m  e  b  d
a  l  a  o  p  c  o  l  o  n  i  e  s  n  g
r  l  n  l  a  u  n  d  r  y  c  p  d  a  e
d  y  t  y  z  o  p  o  s  i  t  i  v  e  v
```

Down

1.
2.
3.
4.
5.
6.
7.
8.

V. Bases and Suffixes.
The spelling list contains fourteen base words and six words with suffixes. Write each spelling word.

Words With Suffixes	Base Words	Words With Suffixes	Base Words
a. positively	_____	k. vacantly	_____
b. auctions	_____	l. awkwardly	_____
c. launching	_____	m. laundries	_____
d. faulty	_____	n. knowledgeable	_____
e. chalky	_____	o. _____	thought
f. squashed	_____	p. _____	lawyer
g. cautioning	_____	q. _____	colony
h. authors	_____	r. _____	astonish
i. paused	_____	s. _____	oppose
j. operas	_____	t. _____	awful

132

Spelling Words

author auction caution fault pause launch laundry thoughtful chalk awfully awkward lawyers opera colonies positive opposite knowledge astonished squash vacant

VI. Not _____, But. Write the spelling word that best fits each phrase.

a. not to continue, but to _____

b. not negative, but _____

c. not ignorance, but _____

d. not an editor, but an _____

e. not the ironing, but the _____

f. not carelessly, but with _____

g. not a concert, but an _____

h. not unthinking, but _____

i. not surprised, but _____

j. not the same, but the _____

k. not to land, but to _____

l. not beans, but _____

m. not graceful, but _____

n. not judges, but _____

o. not wonderfully, but _____

p. not a store sale, but an _____

q. not crayons, but _____

r. not a skill, but a _____

s. not beehives, but ant _____

t. not filled, but _____

VII. Word Parts. Add ending word parts from the box to complete six spelling words. Write the words.

thor	tion	dry	ful	cant	ward

a. auc + _____ = _____

b. thought + _____ = _____

c. va + _____ = _____

d. au + _____ = _____

e. awk + _____ = _____

f. laun + _____ = _____

VIII. All in a Sentence. Use each of the spelling words in sentences about one of the following titles. You may use **Other Word Forms** (p. 131). Circle the spelling words and the other word forms you used.

<u>The Underwater Cave</u> or <u>The Lost Baseball</u>

IX. Final Test. Write each spelling word.

I. Check Test. Write each spelling word.

II. Spelling Words and Phrases

doubt	without a **doubt**
account	a bank **account**
towel	**towel** rack
powerful	a **powerful** motor
approve	will **approve** the changes
improvement	saw the **improvement**
woolen	**woolen** sweater
fully	agreed **fully**
bushel	**bushel** basket
cushion	soft **cushion**
document	a legal **document**
glitter	the gold's **glitter**
differ	seemed to **differ**
familiar	similar and **familiar**
connection	in **connection** with
concerned	a very **concerned** friend
harmony	in perfect **harmony**
expose	to **expose** to the sun
assigned	**assigned** work
muscle	flexed a **muscle**

III. Find a Fit. Write each word in its correct shape.

a.

b.

c.

d.

e.

f.

g.

h.

i.

j.

k.

l.

m.

n.

o.

p.

q.

r.

s.

t.

Other Word Forms

doubted, doubtful, accounts, accounting, accountant, towels, power, powerfully, approved, approving, approval, improve, improved, improving, wool, full, bushels, cushions, cushioned, documentary, glittered, glittery, differed, different, familiarize, connected, connecting, concerning, harmonize, harmonious, exposes, exposing, exposure, assign, assignment, muscles, muscular

135

IV. Generally Speaking. Write the spelling word in the group it best fits.

a. bank record, deposit, _____

b. 4 pecks, 32 quarts, _____

c. record, certificate, _____

d. mistrust, question, _____

e. uncover, lay open, _____

f. completely, wholly, _____

g. placed, appointed, _____

h. washcloth, blanket, _____

i. correction, change, _____

j. body tissue, strength, _____

k. silk, cotton, _____

l. known, common, _____

m. pillow, pad, _____

n. link, union, _____

o. melody, song, _____

p. accept, OK, _____

q. strong, forceful, _____

r. vary, disagree, _____

s. shine, sparkle, _____

t. troubled, worried, _____

V. Guide Words. These word pairs are guide words from the **Glossary/SPELLEX®**. Write the words from the spelling list that appear on the same page as each pair of guide words.

abandon—adventure

1. _____

advertise—assign

2. _____

assigned—boil

3. _____

boiler—chalk

4. _____

concern—cushion

5. _____

6. _____

7. _____

desire—document

8. _____

9. _____

doubt—estate

10. _____

evil—fault

11. _____

12. _____

favor—future

13. _____

gallop—height

14. _____

15. _____

hesitate—insect

16. _____

minor—nowhere

17. _____

power—publish

18. _____

theater—treat

19. _____

vary—wrench

20. _____

Spelling Words

doubt account towel powerful approve improvement woolen fully bushel cushion document glitter differ familiar connection concerned harmony expose assigned muscle

VI. Crossword Puzzle. Solve the puzzle by using all the words from the spelling list. Check your answers in the **Glossary/SPELLEX**®.

Across

4. of wool
5. to be unsure
8. to lay open; uncover
9. to be unalike
11. a bank record
17. completely
18. worried
19. to OK
20. used to dry dishes

Down

1. a link
2. to sparkle
3. provides arm movement
6. something better
7. an official paper
10. known
12. a soft pillow
13. appointed; placed
14. four pecks
15. strong
16. a blending of musical sounds

137

VII. Hidden Words. Read each sentence to find clues to the hidden spelling words. Circle the word hidden in each set of underlined words. Write each word.

a. Each doctor works to <u>improve</u> <u>mental</u> health. _____

b. Thomas <u>signed</u> the <u>completed</u> homework paper. _____

c. From the largest <u>bush</u> <u>eleven</u> baskets of fruit were gathered. _____

d. We installed new showers <u>to</u> <u>welcome</u> the players. _____

e. We <u>wondered</u> <u>if</u> <u>fertile</u> soils vary in mineral content. _____

VIII. Write Your Journal. Use each of the spelling words or **Other Word Forms** (p. 135) to write a page in your journal about the day school was cancelled. Circle the spelling words and the other word forms you used.

IX. Final Test. Write each spelling word.

Lesson 35

I. Check Test. Write each spelling word.

II. Spelling Words and Phrases

cultivate	hard to **cultivate**
separate	**separate** tables
decorate	will **decorate** the room
hesitate	made me **hesitate**
relative	not a close **relative**
election	**election** of the mayor
selection	a varied **selection**
direction	which **direction** to take
inspection	**inspection** time for cars
attention	**attention** to detail
invention	a simple **invention**
convention	political **convention**
assembly	a student **assembly**
amendment	to make an **amendment**
vegetable	a fresh **vegetable**
necessary	**necessary** to do
telegraph	**telegraph** message
telephone	my own **telephone**
television	the **television** program
against	leaned **against** the wall

III. Find a Fit. Write each word in its correct shape.

a.
b.
c.
d.
e.
f.
g.
h.
i.
j.
k.
l.
m.
n.
o.
p.
q.
r.
s.
t.

Other Word Forms

cultivated, cultivating, cultivation, separating, separation, decorating, decoration, decorator, hesitated, hesitation, relate, relating, relation, elect, elected, select, direct, directed, director, inspect, inspected, inspector, attend, attentive, invented, inventor, conventions, assemble, assembling, assemblies, amend, amended, vegetables, necessarily, telegraphed, telephoning, televise, televisions

IV. Word Riddles. Answer each question with a <u>tion</u>, <u>tele</u>, or an <u>ate</u> word from the spelling list.

a. What <u>tion</u> tells how? _____

b. What <u>tion</u> is a close look? _____

c. What <u>tion</u> is a large meeting? _____

d. What <u>tion</u> selects our leaders? _____

e. What <u>tion</u> is careful listening? _____

f. What <u>tion</u> is a choice? _____

g. What <u>tion</u> is something new? _____

h. What <u>tele</u> calls a friend? _____

i. What <u>tele</u> entertains? _____

j. What <u>tele</u> sends a message? _____

k. What <u>ate</u> is to pause? _____

l. What <u>ate</u> is to plow soil? _____

m. What <u>ate</u> is to make a pretty room? _____

n. What <u>ate</u> is to divide? _____

Write the six words that were not used above.

o. _____   q. _____   s. _____

p. _____   r. _____   t. _____

V. Be a Word Detective. Find the missing vowels and write the spelling words.

a. __ g __ __ nst   _____

b. s __ p __ r __ te   _____

c. __ m __ ndm __ nt   _____

d. v __ g __ t __ bl __   _____

e. c __ nv __ nt __ __ n   _____

f. __ l __ ct __ __ n   _____

g. c __ lt __ v __ t __   _____

h. s __ l __ ct __ __ n   _____

i. t __ l __ gr __ ph   _____

j. t __ l __ v __ s __ __ n _____

k. r __ l __ t __ v __   _____

l. d __ r __ ct __ __ n   _____

Spelling Words

cultivate separate decorate hesitate relative election selection direction inspection attention invention convention assembly amendment vegetable necessary telegraph telephone television against

VI. Guide Words. These word pairs are guide words from the **Glossary/SPELLEX®.** Write the words from the spelling list that appear on the same page as each pair of guide words.

advertise—assign

1. _____
2. _____
3. _____

assigned—boil

4. _____

concern—cushion

5. _____
6. _____

customer—design

7. _____

desire—document

8. _____

doubt—estate

9. _____

hesitate—insect

10. _____

insects—knowledge

11. _____
12. _____

minor—nowhere

13. _____

regard—scarce

14. _____

scarcely—sicken

15. _____
16. _____

sudden—terror

17. _____
18. _____
19. _____

vary—wrench

20. _____

141

VII. Building Sentences. Write the following phrases in sentences.

a. yearly convention
b. local election
c. rotten vegetable
d. colored television
e. had to separate
f. school assembly
g. dead telephone
h. secret amendment
i. special inspection
j. can cultivate a garden
k. dangerous invention
l. complete attention
m. will hesitate too long
n. wrong direction
o. against the wind
p. interesting selection
q. completely necessary
r. distant relative
s. telegraph operator
t. will decorate the costume

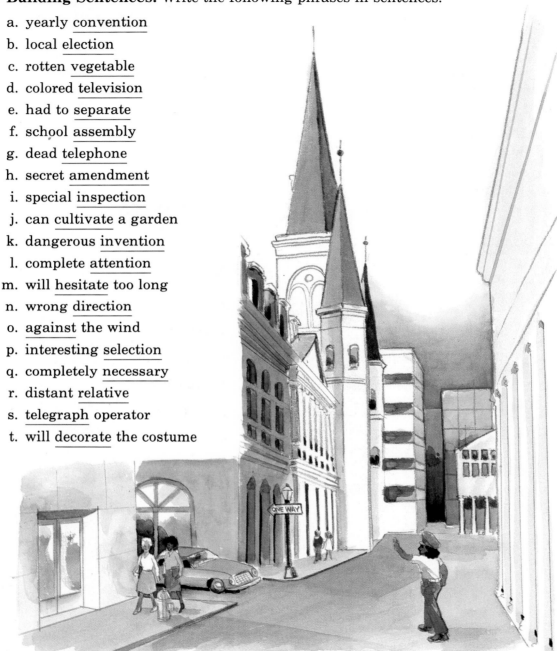

VIII. Final Test. Write each spelling word.

1	2	3	4	5
amendment	differ	fully	opposite	represent
awkward	election	inspection	pause	skeleton
bushel	element	invention	pity	strict
connection	extent	launch	powerful	victory
decorate	fault	memory	relative	woolen

I. Break the Code. Use the code to write an other word form for each spelling word. Write each word.

a	b	c	d	e	f	g	h	i	j	k	l	m
↕	↕	↕	↕	↕	↕	↕	↕	↕	↕	↕	↕	↕
z	y	x	w	v	u	t	s	r	q	p	o	n

a. vovnvmgh — elements

b. rmhkvxgvw — inspected

c. yfhsvoh — bushels

d. hgirxgob — strictly

e. xlmmvxgvw — connected

f. rmevmgrmt — inventing

g. ufoo — full

h. kzfhvh — pauses

i. lkklhv — oppose

j. znvmwvw — amended

k. hpvovgzo — skeletal

l. krgrvh — pities

m. ozfmxsrmt — launching

n. ivkivhvmgvw — represented

o. wvxlizgrlm — decoration

p. wruuvivmg — different

q. zdpdziwob — awkwardly

r. erxglirlfh — victorious

s. nvnlirav — memorize

t. kldviufoob — powerfully

u. vovxgh — elects

v. dllob — wooly

w. ivozgvw — related

x. uzfogh — faults

y. vcgvmwvw — extended

36

1	2	3	4	5
membership	envelope	century	exercise	settlement
selection	activity	dictionary	laundry	delivery
against	lawyers	vegetable	provisions	towel
positive	telegraph	assembly	opera	glitter
squash	mineral	improvement	assigned	muscle

II. Raising Questions. Complete each question by writing other word forms or the spelling words. The number tells you in what column you can find the spelling word. Use each word or its other word form only once. If you need help, use the **Glossary/SPELLEX®**.

a. Were the _____ given sealed _____ to open?
  ₁ ... ₂

b. How many _____ have passed since the Pilgrims _____
  ₃ ... ₅
  in Plymouth?

c. Are gymnastic _____ one of the _____ offered
  ₄ ... ₂
  after school?

d. Were the _____ for the English class _____ on time?
  ₃ ... ₅

e. Did you _____ ripe _____ from the garden?
  ₁ ... ₃

f. Why did the _____ bring his dirty _____ to court?
  ₂ ... ₄

g. Are the wet _____ hanging _____ the wall?
  ₅ ... ₁

h. In 1844, did government officials _____ to watch as Samuel Morse
  ₃
  _____ his first message?
  ₂

i. Is the hotel manager _____ certain that he can _____
  ₁ ... ₄
  all the food?

j. Was the _____ singer wearing _____ or cucumbers
  ₄ ... ₁
  on her hat?

k. Did anyone in the science class know why the stones and _____
  ₂
  were _____ in the dark?
  ₅

l. Has the teacher asked you to _____ your written _____
  ₃ ... ₄
  on the _____ system?
  ₅

1	2	3	4	5
vacant	hesitate	elevator	cultivate	business
approve	chalk	prisoner	awfully	caution
cement	cushion	misery	presented	direction
citizen	telephone	continue	prevent	submit
doubt	arrest	thoughtful	separate	account

III. Sentences in Paragraphs. Write other word forms or the spelling words to complete the blanks. Use the words from column 1 to complete paragraph 1, and so on. Write each word or its other form only once. If you need help, use the **Glossary/SPELLEX®.**

1. While the old hotel is crumbling, its _____ sign still hangs proudly. The holes in the walls provide homes for woodland animals. The mayor of the town has _____ a plan to have all the holes _____ . Yet, concerned _____ are expressing their _____ about this plan because they fear the animals will be injured.

2. The thieves _____ to steal the supplies of _____ from the school. They had already taken _____ and _____ from the school lobby and were afraid of being _____ .

3. All of the _____ stopped with a jolt. We imagined ourselves as _____ with no escape. It was a _____ feeling at first, but we _____ to _____ positively about being rescued.

4. Farmers work very hard _____ their land. Frequently, the _____ problem of having a poor mixture of soil _____ itself. When it is time to plant the crops, delays are _____ by first _____ the soil.

5. When dealing with all customers and _____ , bankers are very _____ . They often guide and _____ borrowers in the _____ of forms to apply for loans. Also, they check to make sure the numbers of all _____ are correct.

36

1	2	3	4	5
familiar	enemies	independent	auction	colonies
express	document	several	reckless	impossible
colony	ability	convention	expose	harmony
stingy	simply	division	necessary	concerned
attention	astonished	author	admission	television

IV. S-t-r-e-t-c-h the Meaning. Write other word forms or the spelling words to stretch the words and their meanings. The number tells you in what column you can find the spelling word. Write each word or its other word form only once. If you need help, use the **Glossary/SPELLEX**®.

a. places where old, _____ items are sold: _____
   (1)   (4)

b. a person who _____ bad feelings: _____
   (1)   (2)

c. a place where early settlers sought _____: _____
   (3)   (5)

d. _____ that permit you to test all of your _____ at
   (2)   (2)
   catching minnows: fishing licenses

e. public meetings where _____ candidates are selected:
   (3)
   _____
   (3)

f. a _____ math operation that gives you half the value of a number:
   (2)
   _____ by two
   (3)

g. singing more than one musical chord that is an _____ without two
   (5)
   or more voices: _____
   (5)

h. people who had _____ about settling in early America:
   (5)
   _____
   (1)

i. the behavior of one who does not spend money _____:
   (4)
   _____
   (1)

j. people who _____ to the matter of writing: _____
   (1)   (3)

k. an act by a magician who never _____ the secret to the audience:
   (4)
   _____ trick
   (2)

l. one of life's _____: food
   (4)

m. devices that display images on a screen: _____
   (5)

n. a place you first go when entering a hospital: _____ room
   (4)

146

SPELLEX® Glossary
Level F

This section of your spelling book is called **SPELLEX® Glossary—Level F.** It is a collection of the spelling words from **Working Words in Spelling—Level F,** together with the phonetic spelling, part of speech, definition, sample phrase, and other word forms for each spelling word.

The **SPELLEX® Glossary** is a useful tool for your spelling work and your everyday writing. It is a valuable resource when doing your spelling exercises and when practicing and reviewing your spelling words. From the groups of other word forms, you can choose the best words to express your ideas or to add variety and smoothness to your writing. The **SPELLEX® Glossary** gives you a quick way to check the spellings and meanings of words.

The **SPELLEX® Glossary** is arranged very simply. All the entry words are listed in alphabetical order. All the spelling words are printed in dark type. If the spelling word is not a base word, you are told what the base word is. With the base word and its definition, you will find the other word forms.

Example: **invitation** |ĭn′vĭ tā′shən| *n.* A polite request to come somewhere: *an invitation to visit.* [see *invite*]

        invite|ĭn vīt′| *v.* To ask someone politely to come somewhere: *will invite them to dinner.* **invites, invited, inviting, invitation, invitations**

PRONUNCIATION KEY

ă	pat	j	**judge**	sh	**dish, ship**
ā	**aid, fey, pay**	k	**cat, kick, pique**	t	**tight**
â	**air, care, wear**	l	**lid, needle**	th	**path, thin**
ä	**father**	m	**am, man, mum**	*th*	**bathe, this**
b	**bib**	n	**no, sudden**	ŭ	**cut, rough**
ch	**church**	ng	**thing**	û	**circle, firm, heard,**
d	**deed**	ŏ	**horrible, pot**		**term, turn, urge, word**
ĕ	**pet, pleasure**	ō	**go, hoarse, row, toe**	v	**cave, valve, vine**
ē	**be, bee, easy, leisure**	ô	**alter, caught, for, paw**	w	**with**
f	**fast, fife, off, phase, rough**	oi	**boy, noise, oil**	y	**yes**
g	**gag**	ou	**cow, out**	yōo	**abuse, use**
h	**hat**	ŏŏ	**took**	z	**rose, size, xylophone, zebra**
hw	**which**	ōō	**boot, fruit**	zh	**garage, pleasure, vision**
ĭ	**pit**	p	**pop**	ə	**about, silent, pencil,**
ī	**by, guy, pie**	r	**roar**		**lemon, circus**
î	**dear, deer, fierce, mere**	s	**miss, sauce, see**	ər	**butter**

STRESS
Primary stress ′ **bi·ol′o·gy** |bī ŏl′ə jē| Secondary stress ′ **bi′o·log′i·cal** |bī′ə lŏj′ĭ kəl|

A

abandon |ə băn′dən| v. **1.** To leave or desert: *to abandon the car.* **2.** To give up completely: *will abandon the old idea.* **abandons, abandoned, abandoning, abandonment**

ability |ə bĭl′ĭ tē| n. The talent to do something; skillfulness: *excellent ability.* **abilities**

abroad |ə brôd′| adv. Outside one's land; to a foreign place: *will travel abroad.*

accent |ăk′sĕnt′| n. A way of pronunciation in a certain area of a country: *a northern accent.* **accents, accented, accenting**

accept |ăk sĕpt′| v. To receive what is offered or given; agree to take: *will accept the gift.* **accepts, accepted, accepting, acceptable, acceptably, acceptant, acceptance, acceptability, accepter**

accident |ăk′sĭ dənt| n. Something unfortunate that happens: *a train accident.* **accidents, accidental, accidentally**

accord |ə kôrd′| v. To be in agreement with: *if the stories accord with each other.* **accords, accorded, according, accordingly, accordance**

according |ə kôr′dĭng| —**According to**—As stated by; as shown by. [see *accord*]

account |ə kount′| n. A record of money saved, exchanged, or owed: *opened an account.* **accounts, accounted, accounting, accountable, accountant**

ache |āk| n. A continuous pain: *a knee ache.* v. To suffer pain; be in pain: *if your legs ache.* **aches, ached, aching**

acid |ăs′ĭd| adj. Sour: *an acid flavor.* n. A compound that gives off hydrogen ions when mixed with water: *the solution of acid.* **acids, acidic, acidly, acidity, acidness**

acre |ā′kər| n. A unit measurement of land area equaling 160 square rods, or 43,560 square feet: *an acre of forest.* **acres, acreage**

action |ăk′shən| n. Motion or activity: *a sudden action.* **actions**

active |ăk′tĭv| adj. **1.** Busy: *an active day.* **2.** Showing much movement: *an active ball game.* **actively, activate, activates, activated, activating, activeness, activity, activities**

activity |ăk tĭv′ĭ tē| n. **1.** An organized event or thing to do: *a school activity.* **2.** An action or motion: *a tiring activity.* [see *active*]

adjust |ə jŭst′| v. **1.** To regulate or put in a position for proper functioning: *to adjust the lens.* **2.** To move into proper position: *to adjust the radio dial.* **adjusts, adjusted, adjusting, adjustable, adjustment, adjuster**

admire |ăd mīr′| v. To look at with wonder or pleasure: *will admire the painting.* **admires, admired, admiring, admiringly, admirable, admirer, admiration**

admission |ăd mĭsh′ən| n. The amount paid for the right to enter: *charged admission.* [see *admit*]

admit |ăd mĭt′| v. **1.** To accept that something is true: *will admit his error.* **2.** To allow in: *to admit several people.* **admits, admitted, admitting, admittedly, admittance, admission, admissions**

adopt |ə dŏpt′| v. **1.** To take as one's own: *to adopt the baby.* **2.** To accept others' ways as one's own: *may adopt their beliefs.* **adopts, adopted, adopting, adoptable, adopter, adoption**

advance |ăd văns′| adj. Early: *an advance warning.* n. A forward motion: *made a very slow advance.* **advances, advanced, advancing, advancer, advancement**

advantage |ăd văn′tĭj| n. Anything that benefits one: *a special advantage.* —**Take advantage of**—To benefit by. **advantages, advantageous, advantageously**

adventure |ăd vĕn′chər| adj. Of or related to an adventure: *saw an adventure movie.* n. A thrilling experience: *a wilderness adventure.* **adventures, adventured, adventuring, adventurer, adventurous, adventurously, adventuresome**

ă pat / ā pay / â care / ä father / ĕ pet / ē be / ĭ pit / ī pie / î fierce / ŏ pot / ō go / ô paw, for / oi oil / ŏŏ book /
ōō boot / ou out / ŭ cut / û fur / th the / th thin / hw which / zh vision / ə ago, item, pencil, atom, circus
©1977 by Houghton Mifflin Company. Reprinted by permission from THE AMERICAN HERITAGE SCHOOL DICTIONARY.

advertise |ăd′vər tīz′| v. To announce publicly the good qualities of something in order to help its sale: *will advertise the bicycles.* **advertises, advertised, advertising, advertisement, advertiser**

advice |ăd vīs′| n. A suggestion or opinion about doing something: *helpful advice.* [see *advise*]

advise |ăd vīz′| v. To offer advice or give an opinion: *will advise them.* **advises, advised, advising, adviser, advice**

affect |ə fĕkt′| v. To change or influence: *can't affect the weather.* —|ăf′ĕkt| n. Feeling or emotion: *showed a great deal of affect.* **affects, affected, affecting**

against |ə gĕnst′| prep. **1.** To touch or come in contact with: *rubs against the car.* **2.** In a direction opposite to: *against the rain.*

agree |ə grē′| v. To be in harmony with: *will agree with you.* **agrees, agreed, agreeing, agreeable, agreeably, agreeableness, agreement, agreements, agreeability**

agreement |ə grē′mənt| n. An understanding between people or nations: *reached an agreement.* [see *agree*]

amend |ə mĕnd′| v. To change a bill, law, or motion by adding, omitting, or changing its wording: *to amend the law.* **amends, amended, amending, amendable, amendment, amendments, amender**

amendment |ə mĕnd′mənt| n. A change made in a law, bill, or motion by adding, omitting, or changing its wording: *an amendment to the rules.* [see *amend*]

amuse |ə myōōz′| v. To make smile or to entertain: *to amuse with toys and games.* **amuses, amused, amusing, amusable, amusement, amusements**

amusement |ə myōōz′mənt| n. Anything that entertains: *a brief, playful amusement.* —**Amusement park**—A park offering many forms of entertainment for profit. [see *amuse*]

anxious |ăngk′shəs| adj. Feeling uneasy or worried: *anxious thoughts.* **anxiously, anxiousness, anxiety, anxieties**

appeal |ə pĕl′| n. An urgent request: *an appeal for food.* **appeals, appealed, appealing, appealingly, appealer**

appear |ə pîr′| v. To come into sight: *will soon appear down in the street.* **disappear, disappears, disappeared, disappearing, disappearance**

approve |ə prōōv′| v. To accept as satisfactory: *to approve the letter.* **approves, approved, approving, approvable, approval, approvals, approver**

area |âr′ē ə| n. A flat, open space: *a play area.* **areas**

argue |är′gyōō| v. To disagree: *will argue among themselves.* **argues, argued, arguing, argument, arguments, argumentative**

argument |är′gyə mənt| n. A disagreement: *a foolish argument.* [see *argue*]

armor |är′mər| n. A metal or leather covering worn to protect the body in battle: *dressed in armor.* **armors, armored, armory**

arrange |ə rānj′| v. To put in order: *to arrange the new books.* **arranges, arranged, arranging, arranger, arrangement, arrangements**

arrangement |ə rānj′mənt| n. Something arranged in a certain way: *a colorful flower arrangement.* [see *arrange*]

arrest |ə rĕst′| n. A holding of a person by authority of the law: *the criminal's arrest.* —**Under arrest**—Held by the police. **arrests, arrested, arresting, arrester**

arrive |ə rīv′| v. To appear or come: *will arrive soon.* **arrives, arrived, arriving, arrival**

article |är′tĭ kəl| n. A written story, complete in itself, on a specific subject but included as part of a magazine, book, or newspaper: *an article on birds.* **articles**

assemble |ə sĕm′bəl| v. To call together or gather: *to assemble all the students.* **assembles, assembled, assembling, assemblage, assembly, assemblies, assembler**

assembly |ə sĕm′blē| n. A calling together of people for a special purpose; a meeting: *an assembly of lawyers.* [see *assemble*]

assign |ə sīn′| v. **1.** To give out: *to assign homework.* **2.** To appoint to: *to assign seats.* **assigns, assigned, assigning, assignable, assigner, assignment**

assigned |ə sīnd'| *v.* **1.** Gave out: *assigned tasks.* **2.** Appointed; placed: *assigned to the front row.* [see *assign*]

assist |ə sĭst'| *v.* To help; aid: *to assist the doctor.* **assists, assisted, assisting, assistant, assistance**

astonish |ə stŏn'ĭsh| *v.* To amaze or surprise: *will astonish the child.* **astonishes, astonished, astonishing, astonishingly, astonishment**

astonished |ə stŏn'ĭsht| *adj.* Amazed or surprised: *astonished crowd.* [see *astonish*]

athlete |ăth'lēt'| *n.* A person trained in physical exercise: *a strong athlete.* **athletes, athletic, athletics**

attain |ə tān'| *v.* To achieve or reach by effort: *to attain greatness.* **attains, attained, attaining, attainable, attainment, attainer**

attend |ə tĕnd'| *v.* To give thought to: *to attend to the matter.* **attends, attended, attending, attentive, attentively, attentiveness, attendance, attendant, attention, attentions**

attention |ə tĕn'shən| *n.* **1.** Thought or focus: *attention to facts.* **2.** Mental concentration on someone or something: *to pay careful attention.* [see *attend*]

attract |ə trăkt'| *v.* To appeal to; be pleasing to: *will attract children.* **attracts, attracted, attracting, attractive, attractively, attractiveness, attraction**

attractive |ə trăk'tĭv| *adj.* Appealing or pleasing: *an attractive shirt.* [see *attract*]

auction |ôk'shən| *n.* A sale in which objects are sold to the person who offers the most money for them: *an auction of antiques.* **auctions, auctioned, auctioning, auctioneer**

author |ô'thər| *n.* A person who writes: *author of novels.* **authors, authored, authoring, authorial**

avoid |ə void'| *v.* To stay away from: *will avoid the ditch.* **avoids, avoided, avoiding, avoidable, avoidably, avoidance**

awful |ô'fəl| *adj.* Bad or frightening: *an awful accident.* **awfully, awfulness**

awfully |ô'fəl lē| *adv.* **1.** Badly: *drove awfully.* **2.** INFORMAL—Very much: *awfully active.* [see *awful*]

awkward |ôk'wərd| *adj.* Clumsy in movement: *an awkward little puppy.* **awkwardly, awkwardness**

B

balance |băl'əns| *v.* To put or hold in a steady position or condition: *to balance the weights.* *n.* A steady position or condition: *an even balance.* **balances, balanced, balancing, balancer**

bargain |bâr'gĭn| *n.* An agreement: *a fair bargain between us.* **bargains, bargained, bargaining, bargainer**

bathe |bāth| *v.* To wash: *will bathe the child.* **bathes, bathed, bathing, bath, bather**

battery |băt'ə rē| *n.* **1.** A single dry cell: *a light's battery.* **2.** A set of electric cells that supplies electric current: *a truck's battery.* **batteries**

behave |bĭ hāv'| *v.* To control oneself; act: *to behave like an adult.* **behaves, behaved, behaving, behavior, behavioral, behaviorally**

beneath |bĭ nēth'| *prep.* In a place below; under: *beneath the table.*

berry |bĕr'ē| *n.* A small, fleshy fruit: *a wild berry.* **berries**

bicycle |bī'sĭk'əl| *n.* A metal vehicle with two wheels and a seat: *a red bicycle.* *adj.* Of or related to a bicycle: *a bicycle tire.* **bicycles, bicycled, bicycling, bicycler, bicyclist**

bluff |blŭf| *n.* Something done or said to fool others: *a difficult bluff.* **—Call one's bluff—** To ask for proof or to challenge someone's actions when trickery is suspected. **bluffs, bluffed, bluffing, bluffer**

boil |boil| *v.* To bubble and give off steam due to heating: *to boil the water.* **boils, boiled, boiling, boiler, boilers**

ă **pat** / ā **pay** / â **care** / ä **father** / ĕ **pet** / ē **be** / ĭ **pit** / ī **pie** / î **fierce** / ŏ **pot** / ō **go** / ô **paw, for** / oi **oil** / o͝o **book** /
o͞o **boot** / ou **out** / ŭ **cut** / û **fur** / *th* **the** / th **thin** / hw **which** / zh **vision** / ə **ago, item, pencil, atom, circus**
©1977 by Houghton Mifflin Company. Reprinted by permission from THE AMERICAN HERITAGE SCHOOL DICTIONARY.

boiler |boi′lər| *n.* A storage tank for heating and holding hot water for a building: *a boiler in the basement.* [see *boil*]

borrow |bŏr′ō| *v.* To use or take something, knowing it must be returned: *will borrow the tools.* **borrows, borrowed, borrowing, borrower**

borrowed |bŏr′ōd| *v.* Used something, knowing it must be returned: *borrowed her book.* [see *borrow*]

breathe |brē*th*| *v.* To take air into the lungs and force it out: *to breathe easily.* **breathes, breathed, breathing, breathable, breather, breath**

brief |brēf| *adj.* Short; quick: *a brief speech.* **briefs, briefed, briefing, briefness, briefer, briefest, briefly**

broad |brôd| *adj.* Wide across: *a broad sidewalk.* **broader, broadest, broaden, broadens, broadened, broadening, broadly, broadness**

burden |bûr′dn| *n.* A load; something carried: *to drop the burden.* **burdens, burdened, burdening, burdensome**

buried |bĕr′ēd| *v.* Hid or covered up: *has buried the bone.* [see *bury*]

bury |bĕr′ē| *v.* To hide or cover up: *to bury gold.* **buries, buried, burying, burial, burier**

bushel |bo͞osh′əl| *n.* A measure for dry goods that equals 4 pecks or 32 quarts: *picked a bushel.* **bushels, busheled, busheling**

business |bĭz′nĭs| *n.* A factory, store, or other commercial establishment; a company: *a major business.* [see *busy*]

busy |bĭz′ē| *adj.* Full of activity: *a busy airport.* **busier, busiest, busies, busied, busying, busyness, business, businesses**

C

cabinet |kăb′ə nĭt| *n.* A compartment or cupboard used for displaying or storing objects: *an empty cabinet.* **cabinets**

ćalendar |kăl′ən dər| *n.* **1.** A list of dates in order of occurrence: *a monthly calendar.* **2.** A chart showing days and months of a particular year: *a wall calendar.* **calendars**

campus |kăm′pəs| *n.* College or school grounds: *a peaceful campus.* **campuses**

capable |kā′pə bəl| *adj.* Able: *two capable ice skaters.* **capably, capableness, capability**

capital |kăp′ĭ tl| *n.* **1.** A city where the government of a state, province, or nation is located: *the state's capital.* **2.** Money or property that is used to increase one's wealth: *not enough capital.* —**Capital letter**— A letter in writing used to begin a sentence or other important words, such as those in book titles. **capitals, capitalize, capitalizes, capitalized, capitalizing, capitalization, capitalist**

capture |kăp′chər| *v.* To take a person or thing by force: *to capture the fort.* **captures, captured, capturing, captive, captivity**

care |kâr| *n.* Caution: *moved with care.* **cares, cared, caring, careful, carefully, carefulness**

carefully |kâr′fəl ē| *adv.* Cautiously: *placed carefully.* [see *care*]

catalog |kăt′l ôg′| *n.* A book containing a list of items and a description of each: *a store catalog.* **catalogs, cataloged, cataloging, cataloger**

caution |kô′shən| *n.* Much care: *looked with caution.* **cautions, cautioned, cautioning, cautionary, cautious, cautiously, cautiousness**

cement |sĭ mĕnt′| *adj.* Of or related to cement: *a cement sidewalk. n.* **1.** A substance used to make concrete and mortar: *paved with cement.* **2.** Anything soft which hardens and causes things to stick together: *a quick-drying cement.* **cements, cemented, cementing, cementer**

century |sĕn′chə rē| *n.* **1.** Each 100 years starting from a particular time: *the seventeenth century.* **2.** One hundred years: *lived for a century.* **centuries**

certain |sûr′tn| *adj.* Showing no doubt; sure: *is certain of these facts.* **uncertain, uncertainly, uncertainty, uncertainness**

chalk |chôk| *n.* A soft substance made from fossil shells, used for writing on a chalkboard: *the teacher's chalk.* **chalks, chalked, chalking, chalky**

chamber |chăm′bər| *n.* A room: *asleep in her own chamber.* **chambers, chambered, chambering**

champion |chăm′pē ən| *n.* The person, thing, or animal that wins a contest or game: *the local sixth-grade spelling champion.* **champions, championed, championing, championship**

channel |chăn′əl| *n.* **1.** A river or stream bed: *a river's channel.* **2.** An airwave of a radio or television station: *switched the channel.* **channels, channeled, channeling**

chapter |chăp′tər| *n.* A division in a book: *my favorite chapter.* **chapters**

charity |chăr′ĭ tē| *n.* A giving to the poor or to an organization that helps the poor, sick, or helpless: *clothes for charity.* **charities, charitable, charitably, charitableness**

charm |chärm| *n.* Appeal or power of pleasing: *has great charm.* **charms, charmed, charming, charmingly, charmer**

charming |chär′mĭng| *adj.* Very appealing: *a charming smile.* [see *charm*]

cheap |chēp| *adj.* Inexpensive; costing very little: *a cheap fare.* **cheaper, cheapest, cheapen, cheapens, cheapened, cheaply, cheapness**

citizen |sĭt′ĭ zən| *n.* **1.** A person who is a member of a nation by choice or by birth: *a U.S. citizen.* **2.** A member of a town or city: *a local citizen.* **citizens, citizenry, citizenship**

claim |klām| *v.* To ask for, insist, or demand as one's own: *to claim the title.* *n.* A demand or request: *made a claim.* **claims, claimed, claiming, claimable, claimant**

claims |klāmz| *v.* Demands, insists, or requests: *claims the box.* *n.* More than one claim: *if several claims are received tomorrow night.* [see *claim*]

coarse |kôrs| *adj.* Rough in texture: *a coarse surface.* **coarser, coarsest, coarsen, coarsened, coarsely, coarseness**

collect |kə lĕkt′| *v.* **1.** To gather or accumulate: *will collect the dirt.* **2.** To bring together to make a set: *to collect old dolls.* **collects, collected, collecting, collectable, collector, collection**

colonies |kŏl′ə nēz| *n.* More than one group of plants or animals living or growing together: *insect colonies.* [see *colony*]

colony |kŏl′ə nē| *n.* **1.** A group of people living together and sharing the same background, occupation, or interest: *a colony of jazz musicians.* **2.** A group of the same kind of plants or animals that live or grow together: *a large ant colony.* **colonies, colonize, colonizes, colonized, colonizing, colonization, colonial, colonially, colonialism, colonist**

command |kə mănd′| *n.* A direction or order: *shouted a command.* *v.* To direct or order: *will command them to leave.* **commands, commanded, commanding, commander, commandment, commandments**

comment |kŏm′ĕnt′| *v.* To make a remark: *will comment on the speech.* *n.* A brief statement or remark about something that has been written, said, or done: *had read the boss's comment.* **comments, commented, commenting, commentator**

common |kŏm′ən| *adj.* Ordinary; usual: *a common plant.* **commoner, commonest, commonly, commonness**

companion |kəm păn′yən| *n.* A person who associates with another; friend: *a childhood companion.* **companions, companionship, companionable**

complete |kəm plēt′| *v.* To finish: *to complete the homework.* **completes, completed, completing, completely, completeness, completion**

compute |kəm pyōōt′| *v.* To find solutions by mathematics or computers: *will compute the answer.* **computes, computed, computing, computerize, computer, computers**

computer |kəm pyōō′tər| *n.* An electronic machine that can store, process, and analyze data: *bought a new computer.* [see *compute*]

ă **pat** / ā **pay** / â **care** / ä **father** / ĕ **pet** / ē **be** / ĭ **pit** / ī **pie** / î **fierce** / ŏ **pot** / ō **go** / ô **paw, for** / oi **oil** / ŏŏ **book** / ōō **boot** / ou **out** / ŭ **cut** / û **fur** / *th* **the** / th **thin** / hw **which** / zh **vision** / ə **ago, item, pencil, atom, circus**
©1977 by Houghton Mifflin Company. Reprinted by permission from THE AMERICAN HERITAGE SCHOOL DICTIONARY.

concern |kən **sûrn'**| *n.* Worry or anxiety: *a look of concern.* **concerns, concerned, concerning, concernment**

concerned |kən **sûrnd'**| *adj.* Troubled; worried: *a concerned mother.* [see *concern*]

concert |**kŏn'**sûrt'| *n.* A musical performance which involves several musicians or singers: *a piano concert.* **concerts, concerto**

confuse |kən **fyōōz'**| *v.* To cause disorder; mix up: *might confuse the drivers.* **confuses, confused, confusing, confusingly, confusedly, confusion**

connect |kə **nĕkt'**| *v.* To join or link one thing to another: *will connect the wires.* **connects, connected, connecting, connective, connector, connection, connections**

connection |kə **nĕk'**shən| *n.* The act of linking one thing to another: *completed the connection.* **—In connection with—**In reference to. [see *connect*]

contain |kən **tān'**| *v.* To hold or have as contents: *does contain art supplies.* **contains, contained, containing, containable, container, containment**

contemplate |**kŏn'**təm plāt'| *v.* To think about: *will contemplate the problem.* **contemplates, contemplated, contemplating**

continent |**kŏn'**tə nənt| *n.* One of the seven largest land masses on earth: *the continent of Asia.* **continents, continental**

continue |kən **tĭn'**yōō| *v.* To keep going: *will continue to walk.* **continues, continued, continuing, continuous, continuously, continual, continually, continuation, discontinue, discontinues, discontinued, discontinuing**

contribute |kən **trĭb'**yōōt| *v.* To give: *will contribute ten dollars.* **contributes, contributed, contributing, contributor, contribution**

convention |kən **vĕn'**shən| *n.* A meeting arranged for a special purpose: *a sales convention.* **conventions**

convince |kən **vĭns'**| *v.* To cause to believe; persuade: *to convince them of the truth.* **convinces, convinced, convincing, convincingly**

cooperate |kō ŏp'ə rāt'| *v.* To work or act together with others: *will cooperate with him.* **cooperates, cooperated, cooperating, cooperative, cooperatively, cooperator, cooperativeness, cooperation**

countries |**kŭn'**trēz| *n.* More than one country: *war between two Asian countries.* [see *country*]

country |**kŭn'**trē| *n.* A nation: *a new country.* **countries**

courage |**kûr'**ĭj| *n.* Bravery: *a medal for courage.* **courageous, courageously**

creature |**krē'**chər| *n.* **1.** Something created: *a make-believe creature.* **2.** A living person or animal: *a lonely creature.* **creatures**

credit |**krĕd'**ĭt| *n.* Reputation or honor: *to one's credit.* *v.* To charge an amount, which will be paid at a later time: *will credit the sale.* **credits, credited, crediting**

creep |krēp| *v.* To move slowly; crawl: *to creep past the door.* **creeps, crept, creeping, creepy, creepier, creepiest, creepily, creepiness, creeper**

cruel |krōō'əl| *adj.* Causing pain: *was a cruel experience for all of us.* **crueler, cruelest, cruelly, cruelty, cruelness**

cultivate |**kŭl'**tə vāt'| *v.* To grow: *will cultivate the corn crop.* **cultivates, cultivated, cultivating, cultivation, cultivator**

cunning |**kŭn'**ĭng| *n.* Slyness or cleverness: *showed much cunning.* *adj.* Sly or clever: *cunning animal in the woods.* **cunningly, cunningness**

curious |**kyōōr'**ē əs| *adj.* Eager to know something: *a curious student.* **curiously, curiosity, curiousness**

curtain |**kûr'**tn| *n.* Cloth hung at windows: *pulled back the white curtain.* **curtains, curtained**

curve |kûrv| *n.* **1.** A bend: *a curve in the driveway.* **2.** A line without a straight part; arc: *to draw a curve.* **curves, curved, curving**

cushion |**kōōsh'**ən| *n.* A soft pad or pillow: *a thick cushion.* **cushions, cushioned, cushioning**

customer |kŭs′tə mər| *n.* A person who purchases something: *a satisfied customer.* ***customers***

D

damage |dăm′ĭj| *n.* Injury that decreases value or usefulness: *damage from the flood.* *v.* To cause injury so as to decrease value or usefulness: *might damage the spare tire.* ***damages, damaged, damaging, damageable***

danger |dān′jər| *n.* The chance or risk of harm: *close to danger.* ***dangers, dangerous, dangerously***

dangerous |dān′jər əs| *adj.* Likely to be harmful: *a dangerous voyage.* [see *danger*]

debate |dĭ bāt′| *n.* An argument which gives reasons for and against: *a loud debate.* *v.* To discuss reasons for and against: *to debate a topic.* ***debates, debated, debating, debatable***

debt |dĕt| *n.* **1.** The condition of owing someone: *one-hundred dollars in debt.* **2.** Something owed: *a large debt.* ***debts, debtor***

decent |dē′sənt| *adj.* Proper: *a decent life.* ***decently, decency***

declare |dĭ klâr′| *v.* To state publicly or formally: *to declare peace.* ***declares, declared, declaring, declarative, declaredly, declarer, declaration***

decline |dĭ klīn′| *v.* To refuse politely: *to decline to go.* ***declines, declined, declining, declinable, decliner***

decorate |dĕk′ə rāt′| *v.* **1.** To paint, paper, furnish, etc., a room: *will decorate the kitchen.* **2.** To make pretty: *will decorate the cake.* ***decorates, decorated, decorating, decorative, decorativeness, decoration, decorator***

defeat |dĭ fēt′| *n.* A loss: *an unexpected defeat.* ***defeats, defeated, defeating, defeatist, defeater***

defend |dĭ fĕnd′| *v.* To protect: *will defend the village.* ***defends, defended, defending, defense, defenses, defensive, defensively, defensiveness, defenseless, defender, defendant***

defense |dĭ fĕns′| *n.* A protection against harm or attack: *defense of the harbor.* [see *defend*]

delight |dĭ līt′| *n.* Great joy: *his delight over the gift.* ***delights, delighted, delighting, delightedly, delightful, delightfully, delightfulness***

delightfully |dĭ līt′fəl ē| *adv.* Very pleasantly: *laughed delightfully.* [see *delight*]

deliver |dĭ lĭv′ər| *v.* To carry and distribute: *will deliver the packages.* ***delivers, delivered, delivering, delivery, deliveries, deliverer***

delivery |dĭ lĭv′ə rē| *adj.* Of or related to a delivery: *delivery service.* *n.* **1.** A carrying and distributing of goods: *made a delivery.* **2.** Something that is delivered: *paid for the delivery.* [see *deliver*]

dentist |dĕn′tĭst| *n.* A doctor who takes care of teeth: *a visit to the dentist.* ***dentists, dental, dentally, dentistry***

department |dĭ pärt′mənt| *n.* A division or part of some whole: *the busy sporting goods department.* ***departments, departmental, departmentally***

deposit |dĭ pŏz′ĭt| *n.* Money put into a bank account: *mailed the deposit.* *v.* To put down: *to deposit his clothes.* ***deposits, deposited, depositing, depositor***

depth |dĕpth| *n.* The distance from top to bottom: *the hole's depth.* ***depths***

deserve |dĭ zûrv′| *v.* To have a right to: *to deserve more credit.* ***deserves, deserved, deserving, deservedly***

design |dĭ zīn′| *n.* A sketch of how something will be made: *a design of the house.* *v.* To draw plans for how something is to be made: *to design a new computer.* ***designs, designed, designing, designer***

ă **pat** / ā **pay** / â **care** / ä **father** / ĕ **pet** / ē **be** / ĭ **pit** / ī **pie** / î **fierce** / ŏ **pot** / ō **go** / ô **paw, for** / oi **oil** / o͞o **book** / o͞o **boot** / ou **out** / ŭ **cut** / û **fur** / *th* **the** / th **thin** / hw **which** / zh **vision** / ə **ago, item, pencil, atom, circus**

desire |dĭ zîr´| v. To want or long for: *to desire some water.* ***desires, desired, desiring, desirous, desirously, desirable, desirably***

dessert |dĭ zûrt´| n. The last course of a meal, often a pastry, fruit, or ice cream: *a sweet dessert.* ***desserts***

destroy |dĭ stroi´| v. To break into pieces or make useless: *will destroy the building.* ***destroys, destroyed, destroying, destroyer, destructive, destruction***

diameter |dĭ ăm´ĭt ər| n. The straight line that passes through the center of a circle or sphere: *measured the diameter.* ***diameters***

diamond |dī´mənd| n. A precious stone formed of pure carbon in crystals: *bought a diamond.* ***diamonds***

dictionary |dĭk´shə nĕr´ē| n. A book that gives information about words, which are arranged in alphabetical order: *the student's dictionary.* ***dictionaries***

diet |dī´ĭt| n. A special selection of foods eaten because of illness or in order to lose or gain weight: *a meatless diet.* ***diets, dieted, dieting, dietary, dietetic, dieter, dietician***

differ |dĭf´ər| v. 1. To be unalike: *to differ in age.* 2. To disagree: *might differ on the two issues.* ***differs, differed, differing, different, differently***

difficult |dĭf´ĭ kŭlt´| adj. Hard to do: *a difficult test.* ***difficultly, difficulty, difficulties***

direct |dĭ rĕkt´| v. 1. To tell or show: *as I direct you.* 2. To lead: *will direct the choir.* ***directs, directed, directing, directly, direction, directions, directional, directness, director, directory, directorship***

directed |dĭ rĕk´tĭd| v. 1. Told or shown: *directed them to their seats.* 2. Led: *directed the band.* [see *direct*]

direction |dĭ rĕk´shən| n. 1. The way in which someone or something faces or points: *in the car's direction.* 2. An instruction or command: *a simple direction.* [see *direct*]

disappear |dĭs´ə pîr´| v. To vanish or pass from sight: *to disappear in the dark.* [see *appear*]

disaster |dĭ zăs´tər| n. A great misfortune that causes much suffering or loss: *a horrible train disaster.* ***disasters, disastrous, disastrously***

discontinue |dĭs´kən tĭn´yoo| v. To end: *will discontinue the game.* [see *continue*]

discuss |dĭ skŭs´| v. To talk over: *will discuss the problem.* ***discusses, discussed, discussing, discussable, discusser, discussion***

disease |dĭ zēz´| n. An illness or infection: *disease of the skin.* ***diseases, diseased***

dislike |dĭs līk´| n. A feeling of not liking: *a dislike of apples.* v. To care little for: *to dislike sports.* [see *like*]

dismiss |dĭs mĭs´| v. To send away or excuse: *will dismiss the army troops.* ***dismisses, dismissed, dismissing, dismissal***

dispute |dĭ spyoot´| n. An argument or debate: *a loud dispute.* ***disputes, disputed, disputing, disputable***

distant |dĭs´tənt| adj. Faraway: *a distant land.* ***distantly, distance***

district |dĭs´trĭkt| n. An area or region: *a farming district.* ***districts***

disturb |dĭ stûrb´| v. 1. To destroy the peace of: *to disturb the quiet.* 2. To bother or annoy: *to disturb with silly questions.* ***disturbs, disturbed, disturbing, disturbingly, disturber, disturbance***

divide |dĭ vīd´| v. 1. To perform the mathematical operation of separating a number into equal parts: *to divide 100 by 50.* 2. To split or separate: *to divide the bread.* ***divides, divided, dividing, divisible, divider, dividend, division, divisions***

division |dĭ vĭzh´ən| n. 1. The mathematical operation of dividing one number by another number: *to learn division.* 2. A part or section: *a division of the company.* 3. Something that keeps separate or divides: *a glass division.* [see *divide*]

document |dŏk´yə mənt| n. An official paper that gives information or proof of some fact: *filed a document for the court case.* ***documents, documented, documenting, documentation, documentary***

doubt |dout| *v.* To be unsure; question: *doesn't doubt his guilt.* —**Without doubt**— Surely or certainly. *doubts, doubted, doubting, doubtingly, doubtable, doubtful, doubtfully, doubtfulness, doubtless, doubtlessly, doubtlessness, doubter*

E

eager |ē′gər| *adj.* Full of impatient curiosity: *an eager learner. eagerly, eagerness*

easy |ē′zē| *adj.* Relaxed; comfortable: *an easy manner. uneasy, uneasier, uneasiest, uneasily, uneasiness*

echo |ĕk′ō| *n.* A repeating of a sound: *his voice's echo. echoes, echoed, echoing*

effort |ĕf′ərt| *n.* A strong attempt: *an effort to finish. efforts, effortless, effortlessly*

elect |ĭ lĕkt′| *v.* To choose for an office by voting: *will elect a president this week. elects, elected, electing, elective, electively, elector, electoral, electorate, election, elections, electioneer*

election |ĭ lĕk′shən| *n.* A choosing for an office by vote: *an election for governor.* [see *elect*]

element |ĕl′ə mənt| *n.* **1.** An important feature: *a necessary element.* **2.** A substance that cannot be broken down chemically: *tested the element. elements*

elevate |ĕl′ə vāt′| *v.* To raise or lift upward: *will elevate the seat. elevates, elevated, elevating, elevation, elevator, elevators*

elevator |ĕl′ə vā′tər| *n.* A platform or cage used to move people or things from one floor to another of a building: *a full elevator.* [see *elevate*]

empire |ĕm′pīr′| *n.* A group of states or nations under one ruler: *a powerful empire. empires, emperor, empress*

enemies |ĕn′ə mēz| *n.* More than one enemy: *many angry enemies.* [see *enemy*]

enemy |ĕn′ə mē| *n.* A person or group of persons that hate and try to hurt each other: *an evil enemy. enemies*

energy |ĕn′ər jē| *n.* Power or fuel for making things work: *solar energy. energies, energetic, energetically, energize, energizes, energized, energizing, energizer*

enforce |ĕn fôrs′| *v.* To force obedience to: *will enforce the rules. enforces, enforced, enforcing, enforceable, enforcer, enforcement*

entertain |ĕn′tər tān′| *v.* To amuse or please: *will entertain the guests. entertains, entertained, entertaining, entertainer, entertainingly, entertainment*

entire |ĕn tīr′| *adj.* Whole or complete: *the entire collection of stamps. entirely, entirety, entireness*

entirely |ĕn tīr′lē| *adv.* Completely: *entirely pleased.* [see *entire*]

envelope |ĕn′və lōp′| *n.* A paper cover with a gummed flap in which a letter or anything flat can be mailed: *an airmail envelope. envelopes*

equal |ē′kwəl| *adj.* The same; even: *equal amounts of flour and water. equals, equaled, equaling, equally, equalize, equality, equalizer*

error |ĕr′ər| *n.* A mistake: *an error in arithmetic. errors, errorless*

establish |ĭ stăb′lĭsh| *v.* **1.** To set up on a lasting basis; found: *will establish a territory.* **2.** To arrange or set up: *to establish a law practice. establishes, established, establishing, establishment*

estate |ĭ stāt′| *n.* **1.** A large piece of property belonging to someone: *a magnificent estate.* **2.** All the objects and property left by a dead person: *left her entire estate to her children. estates*

ă **pat** / ā **pay** / â **care** / ä **father** / ĕ **pet** / ē **be** / ĭ **pit** / ī **pie** / î **fierce** / ŏ **pot** / ō **go** / ô **paw, for** / oi **oil** / ŏŏ **book** / ŏŏ **boot** / ou **out** / ŭ **cut** / û **fur** / *th* **the** / th **thin** / hw **which** / zh **vision** / ə **ago, item, pencil, atom, circus**

evil |ē′vəl| *adj.* Wicked: *evil thoughts.* **eviler, evilest, evilly, evils, evilness**

exact |ĭg zăkt′| *adj.* Correct or accurate; precise: *exact answer.* **exactly, exactness**

exactly |ĭg zăkt′lē| *adv.* Correctly or precisely: *measured exactly.* [see *exact*]

example |ĭg zăm′pəl| *n.* A pattern or model to be imitated: *shown as an example.* **examples**

exchange |ĭks chănj′| *v.* To change or trade for another: *may exchange the blouse.* **exchanges, exchanged, exchanging, exchangeable, exchanger**

excite |ĭk sīt′| *v.* To stir up the emotions of: *will excite the crowd.* **excites, excited, exciting, excitingly, excitedly, excitable, excitably, exciter, excitement**

excitement |ĭk sīt′mənt| *n.* Enthusiasm: *excitement over the race.* [see *excite*]

exclaim |ĭk sklām′| *v.* To speak suddenly or cry out: *to exclaim with surprise.* **exclaims, exclaimed, exclaiming, exclamatory, exclaimer, exclamation**

exercise |ĕk′sər sīz′| *n.* An activity requiring physical exertion to maintain or create fitness: *walked for exercise.* **exercises, exercised, exercising, exerciser**

exhibit |ĭg zĭb′ĭt| *n.* A display or show: *a science exhibit.* *v.* To show or display: *will exhibit the project.* **exhibits, exhibited, exhibiting, exhibition, exhibitor**

expect |ĭk spĕkt′| *v.* To look forward to or think something will happen: *to expect a phone call.* **expects, expected, expecting, expectable, expectant, expectantly, expectedly, expectancy, expectation**

expense |ĭk spĕns′| *n.* The cost or the amount of money spent: *expense of the coat.* **expenses, expensive, expensively, expensiveness**

expensive |ĭk spĕn′sĭv| *adj.* Costly: *a very expensive ring.* [see *expense*]

expert |ĕk′spûrt′| *adj.* Having great skill, experience, or knowledge in a particular subject: *an expert mechanic.* *n.* A person who has great knowledge about some special subject: *an expert on animals.* **experts, expertly, expertness**

explain |ĭk splān′| *v.* To make clear or understandable: *will explain the riddle of the missing doll.* **explains, explained, explaining, explainable, explanatory, explanation**

explore |ĭk splôr′| *v.* To travel or wander through an unfamiliar place: *to explore the cove.* **explores, explored, exploring, exploratory, explorer, exploration**

expose |ĭk spōz′| *v.* To uncover or lay open: *to expose to air.* **exposes, exposed, exposing, exposure, exposer, exposition**

express |ĭk sprĕs′| *n.* A train, bus, etc., that travels fast and makes few stops: *took an express.* *v.* To show by look, voice, or action: *to express sadness.* **expresses, expressed, expressing, expressive, expressiveness, expressively, expression, expressions, expressionless**

extent |ĭk stĕnt′| *n.* **1.** The range of something: *the extent of the damage.* **2.** The distance or area to which a thing extends: *the extent of the property.* **extents, extend, extends, extended, extending, extensive, extension, extender**

extra |ĕk′strə| *adj.* Additional: *an extra layer.* **extras**

F

factories |făk′tə rēz| *n.* More than one factory: *the automobile factories.* [see *factory*]

factory |făk′tə rē| *n.* A building where goods are made: *a busy factory.* **factories**

familiar |fə mĭl′yər| *adj.* Well-known or common: *a familiar book.* **familiarly, familiarize, familiarizes, familiarized, familiarizing, familiarity, familiarities**

farewell |fâr′wĕl′| *n.* The act of saying good-by: *waved a farewell.* **farewells**

fault |fôlt| *n.* **1.** Responsibility for an error: *the fault of the owner.* **2.** A defect or flaw: *its worst fault.* **faults, faulted, faulting, faulty, faultless, faultlessly, faultiness**

favor |fā′vər| v. **1.** To help or benefit: *would favor their needs.* **2.** To like or prefer: *to favor her idea.* **favors, favored, favoring, favorable, favorably, favorableness, favorite, favorites, favoritism**

favorable |fā′vər ə bəl| adj. Positive or pleasing: *a favorable decision.* [see *favor*]

favorite |fā′vər it| adj. Liked best; preferred: *my favorite movie.* [see *favor*]

figure |fĭg′yər| n. **1.** A shape or form: *a dark figure.* **2.** A symbol for a number: *the figure 10.* —**Figure out**—To understand. **figures, figured, figuring, figurine**

final |fī′nəl| adj. Allowing no further actions; decisive: *his final word.* **finals, finally, finalize, finalizes, finalized, finalizing, finalist, finale**

finally |fī′nə lē| adv. At last: *has finally finished.* [see *final*]

firm |fûrm| adj. **1.** Strong and sure: *a firm hold.* **2.** Steady; unshaking: *a firm belief.* **firms, firmed, firming, firmer, firmest, firmly, firmness**

flavor |flā′vər| n. Taste: *a strawberry flavor.* v. To give a taste to: *will flavor the meat.* **flavors, flavored, flavoring, flavorful, flavorfully, flavorsome, flavorless, flavorlessly**

forbid |fər bĭd′| v. Not to allow: *will forbid them to leave.* **forbids, forbade, forbidden, forbidding, forbiddingly, forbiddance**

forbidden |fər bĭd′n| adj. Not allowed: *a forbidden food.* [see *forbid*]

force |fôrs| n. Strength or power: *the force of the explosion.* **forces, forced, forcing, forcible, forcibly, forceful, forcefully, forcefulness**

forehead |fôr′hĕd′| n. The upper part of the face above the eyes: *hit his forehead.* **foreheads**

foreign |fôr′in| adj. **1.** Of or from another country: *foreign food.* **2.** Not belonging or related: *found a foreign object.* **foreigner, foreigners, foreignness**

fortune |fôr′chən| n. Great wealth: *won a fortune.* —**Fortune cookie**— An Oriental cookie which has a saying or a prediction of a fortune written on a piece of paper inside. **fortunes, fortunate, fortunately, fortuneless**

frank |frăngk| adj. Free and open about expressing one's thoughts: *a frank opinion.* **franker, frankest, frankly, frankness**

frankly |frăngk′lē| adv. In an open manner: *expressed frankly.* [see *frank*]

freight |frāt| n. Goods carried by a vessel or vehicle; cargo: *the ship's freight.* **freighter**

fright |frīt| n. Sudden terror: *a look of fright.* **frights, frighten, frightens, frightened, frightening, frighteningly, frightful, frightfully**

frighten |frīt′n| v. To fill with fear: *might frighten the crowd.* [see *fright*]

full |fŏŏl| adj. Unable to hold anymore; filled: *a full glass.* **fuller, fullest, fully, fullness**

fully |fŏŏl′ē| adv. Completely: *fully cooked.* [see *full*]

funeral |fyŏŏ′nər əl| adj. Of or related to a funeral: *a funeral director.* n. The services accompanying the burial or burning of a dead person's body: *a quiet funeral.* **funerals**

furnace |fûr′nĭs| n. An enclosed box in which an intense fire is created to heat buildings or melt metals: *the house's furnace.* **furnaces**

furnish |fûr′nĭsh| v. To supply with furniture or equipment: *will furnish the apartment.* **furnishes, furnished, furnishing, furnishings, furnisher, furniture**

furniture |fûr′nə chər| n. Movable articles such as chairs, tables, etc., which make an area fit for living or working: *arranged the furniture.* [see *furnish*]

future |fyŏŏ′chər| n. The time that is to come: *planned for the future.* adj. Of or related to the future: *a future meeting.* **futures, futuristic**

ă pat / ā pay / â care / ä father / ĕ pet / ē be / ĭ pit / ī pie / î fierce / ŏ pot / ō go / ô paw, for / oi oil / ŏŏ book /
ŏŏ boot / ou out / ŭ cut / û fur / th the / th thin / hw which / zh vision / ə ago, item, pencil, atom, circus
©1977 by Houghton Mifflin Company. Reprinted by permission from THE AMERICAN HERITAGE SCHOOL DICTIONARY.

G

gallop |găl′əp| v. To go very fast: *to gallop away.* **gallops, galloped, galloping, galloper**

garbage |gär′bĭj| adj. Of or related to garbage: *a garbage bag.* n. Anything worthless: *put into the garbage.*

gear |gîr| n. 1. A set of toothed wheels that fit together and often move at different speeds to transmit power: *switched the gear.* 2. Equipment: *packed her hiking gear.* **gears, geared, gearing**

gentle |jĕn′tl| adj. Not violent or rough; mild: *a gentle manner.* **gentler, gentlest, gently, gentleness**

ghost |gōst| n. A dead person's spirit, believed by some to exist: *a ghost in the haunted house.* **ghosts, ghostly**

glance |glăns| n. A brief look: *a shy glance.* v. To look briefly: *a sudden glance.* **glances, glanced, glancing**

glitter |glĭt′ər| n. A sparkling brightness: *the glitter of the water.* v. To sparkle or shine: *will glitter in the light.* **glitters, glittered, glittering, glitteringly, glittery**

gloom |glōōm| n. Darkness; dimness: *full of gloom.* **gloomy, gloomier, gloomiest, gloomily, gloominess**

gloomy |glōō′mē| adj. Dark and dreary: *gloomy weather.* [see *gloom*]

glory |glôr′ē| n. Fame or honor: *tale of the hero's glory.* **glories, glorify, glorifies, glorified, glorifying, glorifier, glorious, gloriously**

gossip |gŏs′əp| n. Idle rumors: *a neighbor's gossip.* **gossips, gossiped, gossiping, gossipy, gossiper**

govern |gŭv′ərn| v. To direct or rule with authority: *to govern the territory.* **governs, governed, governing, governable, governor, government, governments**

government |gŭv′ərn mənt| adj. Of or related to a government: *a government agency.* n. The ruling system of a country, state, district, etc.: *a democratic government.* [see *govern*]

grateful |grāt′fəl| adj. Thankful: *grateful for the gift.* **gratefully, gratefulness**

great |grāt| adj. Large: *a great animal.* **greater, greatest, greatly, greatness**

greater |grā′tər| adj. Larger: *a greater amount.* [see *great*]

grief |grēf| n. Extreme sadness: *tears of grief.* **grieve, grieves, grieved, grieving, grievous, grievance**

groceries |grō′sə rēz| n. Articles of food and supplies sold by a grocer: *delivered the groceries.* [see *grocery*]

grocery |grō′sə rē| n. A store selling food and household items: *fruit from the grocery.* **groceries, grocer**

H

handkerchief |hăng′kər chĭf| n. A small square cloth used to wipe the nose, brow, etc.: *folded the handkerchief.* **handkerchiefs**

happiness |hăp′ē nĭs| n. Gladness: *shouted with happiness.* [see *happy*]

happy |hăp′ē| adj. Pleased or glad: *a happy laugh.* **happier, happiest, happily, happiness**

harmony |här′mə nē| n. 1. Agreement in feeling; good will: *lived in harmony.* 2. A blending together of musical sounds: *to sing in harmony.* **harmonize, harmonizes, harmonized, harmonizing, harmonizer, harmonies, harmonious, harmoniously, harmoniousness, harmonics, harmonist**

haste |hāst| n. Hurry: *made in haste.* **hasten, hastens, hastened, hastening, hasty, hastily**

headache |hĕd′āk′| n. A pain occurring in the head: *sick with a headache.* **headaches**

health |hĕlth| n. The condition of the body or mind: *in perfect health.* **healthy, healthier, healthiest, healthful, healthfully, healthily, healthiness, healthfulness**

healthy |hĕl′thē| adj. Producing or giving health: *a healthy diet.* [see *health*]

height |hīt| n. The measurement from top to bottom of a thing or person: *the man's height.* **heights, heighten, heightens, heightened, heightening**

hesitate |hĕz′ĭ tāt′| v. To pause or hold back: *to hesitate at the door.* **hesitates, hesitated, hesitating, hesitatingly, hesitant, hesitater, hesitation**

high |hī| adj. Greater than others: *at a high cost.* **higher, highest, highly, highness**

highly |hī′lē| adv. Very much or in an extreme degree: *highly intelligent.* [see *high*]

horizon |hə rī′zən| n. The line where the earth and sky appear to meet: *colorful sunset on the horizon.* **horizons, horizontal, horizontally**

human |hyōō′mən| n. A person: *footprints of a human.* adj. Of or relating to people: *human error.* **humans, humanly, humane, humanely, humanitarian, humanity, humanness, humanist, humanism**

humor |hyōō′mər| n. A funny or entertaining quality: *a joke with good humor.* **humors, humored, humoring, humorous, humorously, humorist**

idle |īd′l| adj. Not busy: *an idle worker.* **idles, idled, idling, idly, idleness, idler**

import |ĭm′pôrt′| adj. Of or related to an import: *an import charge.* v. To bring in goods from another country for trade or sale: *to import silk.* **imports, imported, importing, importable, importer, importation**

important |ĭm pôr′tnt| adj. Valuable or necessary: *an important package in the mail.* **importantly, importance**

impossible |ĭm pŏs′ə bəl| adj. Not able to be done: *an impossible math assignment.* [see *possible*]

improve |ĭm prōōv′| v. To make better: *will improve the recipe.* **improves, improved, improving, improvable, improvement, improvements**

improvement |ĭm prōōv′mənt| n. A change or addition for the better: *improvement of the neighborhood.* [see *improve*]

impulse |ĭm′pŭls′| n. A sudden urge: *an impulse to leave for home.* **impulses, impulsive, impulsively**

incline |ĭn klīn′| v. To have a tendency; tend: *incline to eat too fast.* **inclines, inclined, inclining, inclination**

inclined |ĭn klīnd′| adj. Willing; tending: *was inclined to leave.* [see *incline*]

include |ĭn klōōd′| v. To be part of a total amount: *does include the tip.* **includes, included, including, inclusive, inclusion**

income |ĭn′kŭm′| n. The money made from employment, business, property, etc.: *earns a good income.* **incomes, incoming**

increase |ĭn′krēs| n. A gain in amount or size: *a rapid increase in weight.* **increases, increased, increasing, increasingly**

independent |ĭn′dĭ pĕn′dənt| adj. Not depending on others: *began an independent activity.* **independently, independence, independency**

infant |ĭn′fənt| n. A baby or very young child: *carried the infant home.* **infants, infantile, infancy**

injure |ĭn′jər| v. To harm: *to injure an arm.* **injures, injured, injuring, injurious, injurer, injury, injuries**

inning |ĭn′ĭng| n. A division in a baseball game, with a top and a bottom half during which each team has a turn at bat: *the second inning.* **innings**

inquire |ĭn kwīr′| v. To ask about something: *may inquire about the sale.* **inquires, inquired, inquiring, inquiringly, inquiry, inquiries, inquirer, inquisition**

insect |ĭn′sĕkt′| n. One of a large group of small animals without a backbone. It has six legs and a body made up of three main divisions: *insect with wings.* **insects**

ă pat / ā pay / â care / ä father / ĕ pet / ē be / ĭ pit / ī pie / î fierce / ŏ pot / ō go / ô paw, for / oi oil / ōō book / ōō boot / ou out / ŭ cut / û fur / *th* the / th thin / hw which / zh vision / ə ago, item, pencil, atom, circus

insects |ĭn′sĕkts′| *n.* More than one insect: *insects in the garden.* [see *insect*]

insist |in sĭst′| *v.* To state strongly; demand: *to insist they go.* **insists, insisted, insisting, insistent, insistently**

inspect |in spĕkt′| *v.* To examine carefully: *will inspect the room.* **inspects, inspected, inspecting, inspection, inspections, inspector**

inspection |in spĕk′shən| *n.* An examination or close look: *an official inspection.* [see *inspect*]

instant |ĭn′stənt| *n.* A particular moment: *will start working at this very instant.* **instants, instantly, instantaneous, instantaneously, instance**

instead |in stĕd′| *adv.* As a substitute: *had milk instead.* —**Instead of**—In place of; rather than.

instruct |in strŭkt′| *v.* To teach or train: *will instruct the science students.* **instructs, instructed, instructing, instruction, instructions, instructional, instructive, instructor**

instruction |in strŭk′shən| *n.* A lesson or teaching: *skiing instruction.* [see *instruct*]

insure |in shoŏr′| *v.* **1.** To buy insurance for something: *will insure his boat.* **2.** To guarantee: *to insure good credit.* **insures, insured, insuring, insurable, insurer, insurance**

introduce |in′trə doōs′| *v.* **1.** To present someone by name to another or others: *will introduce the new neighbor.* **2.** To make known: *to introduce two new products to the public.* **introduces, introduced, introducing, introductory, introduction**

invent |in vĕnt′| *v.* To think up and create something new: *to invent a new machine.* **invents, invented, inventing, inventive, inventively, inventiveness, invention, inventions, inventional, inventor**

invention |in vĕn′shən| *n.* Something created, or invented, which did not exist before: *a scientific invention.* [see *invent*]

invitation |in′vĭ tā′shən| *n.* A polite request to come somewhere: *an invitation to visit.* [see *invite*]

invite |in vīt′| *v.* To ask someone politely to come somewhere: *will invite them to dinner.* **invites, invited, inviting, invitation, invitations**

issue |ĭsh′oō| *n.* A certain quantity of magazines, newspapers, stamps, etc., sent out or given out at one time: *this month's issue.* *v.* To put out or send forth: *will issue a new set of rules.* **issues, issued, issuing, issuable**

J

jealous |jĕl′əs| *adj.* Full of envy: *a jealous act.* **jealously, jealousy, jealousness**

jewel |joō′əl| *n.* A gem or precious stone: *a valuable jewel.* **jewels, jeweled, jeweling, jewelry, jeweler**

jewels |joō′əlz| *n.* Precious stones: *sparkling like jewels.* [see *jewel*]

joint |joint| *n.* **1.** A place where two parts are connected: *a chair's joint.* **2.** The part of an animal or human where two bones join: *an ankle joint.* **joints, jointed, jointly**

journey |jûr′nē| *n.* A trip: *a long journey.* *v.* To take a trip; travel: *will journey west by bus.* **journeys, journeyed, journeying, journeyer**

jury |joōr′ē| *n.* A group of people chosen to give a judgment about something or someone: *a member of a jury.* **juries, juror**

just |jŭst| *adj.* Fair or honest: *a just law.* **unjust, unjustly, unjustness**

K

knit |nĭt| *v.* To make cloth or clothing by looping yarn or thread together by hand with long needles, or by machine: *to knit a sweater.* *adj.* Of a fabric made by knitting: *a knit suit.* **knits, knitted, knitting, knitter**

knitting |nĭt′ing| *v.* Making cloth by looping yarn or thread together: *is knitting a scarf.* *adj.* Of or related to knitting: *knitting instructions.* *n.* The process of making cloth from knitting: *learned knitting in school.* [see *knit*]

knowledge |nŏl′ ĭj| *n.* Understanding gained through experience or study: *knowledge of ancient cultures.* **knowledgeable**

L

labor |lă′bər| *n.* Work or toil: *proud of their labor.* —**Labor union**—An organization of workers united together to protect their interests. **labors, labored, laboring, laborious, laboriously, laborer**

landlord |lănd′lôrd′| *n.* A person who owns land or buildings to rent to others: *met the landlord.* **landlords**

landscape |lănd′skăp′| *n.* Scene; view: *a breathtaking landscape.* **landscapes, landscaped, landscaping, landscaper**

lantern |lăn′tərn| *n.* A container for holding a light that shines through: *carried a lantern.* **lanterns**

last |lăst| *v.* To continue to exist: *will last for many years.* **lasts, lasted, lasting, lastingly, lastly, lastingness**

lasting |lăs′tĭng| *adj.* Remaining for a long time: *a lasting illness.* [see *last*]

launch |lônch| *v.* To set something in motion: *will launch the satellite.* **launches, launched, launching, launcher**

laundry |lôn′drē| *n.* Clothes, towels, etc., that are washed or need to be washed: *did the laundry.* **laundries, launder, launders, laundered, laundering, launderer, laundromat**

lawyer |lô′yər| *n.* A person trained to give legal advice and to represent clients in court: *hired a lawyer.* **lawyers**

lawyers |lô′yərz| *n.* More than one lawyer: *a meeting of lawyers.* [see *lawyer*]

league |lēg| *adj.* Of a league: *a league player.* *n.* An association of sports teams or clubs: *a baseball league.* **leagues**

lease |lēs| *n.* A written agreement that says how long a particular property is rented and how much money should be paid for it: *a three-year lease.* *v.* To rent: *will lease their house.* **leases, leased, leasing**

length |lĕngkth| *n.* The measure of how long a thing is: *a length of six feet.* **lengths, lengthen, lengthens, lengthened, lengthening, lengthy, lengthier, lengthiest**

lettuce |lĕt′ĭs| *n.* A green garden plant, often used in salads: *fresh lettuce from the garden.*

like |līk| *v.* To enjoy: *to like baseball.* **dislike, dislikes, disliked, disliking, dislikable**

limit |lĭm′ĭt| *v.* To restrict: *may limit his freedom. n.* **1.** An edge or farthest point: *the platform's limit.* **2.** The point beyond which one cannot go or do something: *a speed limit.* **limits, limited, limiting, limitless, limitation**

linen |lĭn′ən| *n.* A cloth or thread made from flax: *bought some linen.* **linens**

liquid |lĭk′wĭd| *n.* A fluid or substance that is neither a solid nor a gas: *a container of hot liquid.* **liquids, liquefy, liquefies, liquefied, liquefying, liquidity, liquidness**

locate |lō′kāt′| *v.* To find by searching or examining: *can't locate the leak.* **locates, located, locating, location**

loss |lôs| *n.* A losing of something; a decrease: *a loss of energy.* **losses**

loyal |loi′əl| *adj.* Faithful: *a loyal employee.* **loyally, loyalty, loyalties, loyalism, loyalist**

M

machine |mə shēn′| *n.* A device used for doing work, each part having a special function: *built a machine.* **machines, machinery, machinist**

ă **pat** / ā **pay** / â **care** / ä **father** / ĕ **pet** / ē **be** / ĭ **pit** / ī **pie** / î **fierce** / ŏ **pot** / ō **go** / ô **paw, for** / oi **oil** / o͝o **book** / o͞o **boot** / ou **out** / ŭ **cut** / û **fur** / th **the** / th **thin** / hw **which** / zh **vision** / ə **ago, item, pencil, atom, circus**
©1977 by Houghton Mifflin Company. Reprinted by permission from THE AMERICAN HERITAGE SCHOOL DICTIONARY.

machinery |mə **shē**′nə rē| *n.* More than one machine: *fixed the machinery.* [see *machine*]

major |**mā**′jər| *adj.* Larger or greater: *a major amount. n.* An officer of the army, air force, or marines: *saluted the major.* **majors, majored, majoring, majority, majorities**

manage |**măn**′ĭj| *v.* To succeed in accomplishing: *will manage to deliver it.* **manages, managed, managing, manageable, manager, management**

manner |**măn**′ər| *n.* A way of doing something: *in an organized manner.* **manners, mannered, mannerly, mannerism**

manual |**măn**′yo͞o əl| *n.* A handbook: *a helpful manual.* **manuals, manually**

manufacture |măn′yə **făk**′chər| *v.* To make something by hand or by machine from raw materials: *to manufacture larger cars and trucks.* **manufactures, manufactured, manufacturing, manufacturer**

manufacturing |măn′yə **făk**′chər ĭng| *adj.* Of or related to manufacturing: *a manufacturing center. n.* The process of making something from raw materials: *the manufacturing of glass.* [see *manufacture*]

margin |**mär**′jĭn| *n.* **1.** The blank space around a printed page: *will keep a straight margin.* **2.** Edge or border: *a margin of ribbon.* **margins, margined, marginal, marginally**

mass |măs| *n.* **1.** A great quantity: *a mass of clouds.* **2.** A lump: *a mass of clay.* **masses, massed, massing, massive**

material |mə **tîr**′ē əl| *n.* **1.** A fabric or cloth: *a soft material.* **2.** What a thing is made from: *material for building.* **materials, materialize, materializes, materialized, materializing**

mean |mēn| *v.* To intend: *to mean nothing.* **means, meant, meaning**

meant |měnt| *v.* Intended: *meant to go.* [see *mean*]

measure |**mězh**′ər| *n.* An amount or size: *a small measure of salt. v.* To find the amount or size of something: *will measure the window.* **measures, measured, measuring, measurable, measurably, measurement**

medicine |**měd**′ĭ sĭn| *n.* A substance, usually a drug, used to treat or prevent disease: *the patient's medicine.* **medicines, medical, medically, medicinal, medicate, medicates, medicated, medicating, medication, medic**

medium |**mē**′dē əm| *adj.* Middle in size, condition, or quality: *was set on medium speed.* **mediums, media, median**

member |**měm**′bər| *n.* Anyone or anything belonging to a group: *a member of the team.* **members, membership, memberships**

membership |**měm**′bər shĭp′| *n.* The state of being a member: *continued her membership.* [see *member*]

memory |**měm**′ə rē| *n.* The ability to remember: *has an excellent memory.* **memories, memorize, memorizes, memorized, memorizing, memorization**

metal |**mět**′l| *adj.* Made of metal: *a metal handle. n.* An element or substance that has a shine and can conduct electricity and heat easily: *a shiny metal.* **metals, metallic**

meter |**mē**′tər| *n.* **1.** A device that measures and records the amount of electricity, gas, water, etc., used: *has read the meter.* **2.** A metric unit of length that equals 39.37 inches: *one meter in length.* **meters, metered, metering, metric**

method |**měth**′əd| *n.* A way of doing something; procedure: *a slow method.* **methods**

middle |**mĭd**′l| *n.* The halfway point; center: *the middle of the room.* **midst, mid**

midst |mĭdst| *prep.* Among: *midst the cartons. n.* The middle: *in the midst of the field.* [see *middle*]

mine |mīn| *v.* To dig for gold, coal, etc.: *will mine for minerals.* **mines, mined, mining, miner, miners**

mineral |**mĭn**′ər əl| *adj.* Containing minerals: *mineral water. n.* A substance, such as coal, gold, or ores, obtained by mining: *a dull mineral.* **minerals, mineralize, mineralizes, mineralized, mineralizing, mineralogy, mineralogist**

mining |**mī**′nĭng| *v.* Digging for gold, coal, etc.: *was mining for gems. adj.* Of or for mining: *mining tools.* [see *mine*]

minor |mī′nər| *adj.* Lesser in importance; smaller: *caused a minor traffic delay.* **minors, minored, minoring, minority, minorities**

misery |mĭz′ə rē| *n.* Unhappiness or suffering: *a sigh of misery.* **miseries, miserable, miserably, miserableness**

motion |mō′shən| *n.* A movement: *a quick motion.* **motions, motioned, motioning, motionless**

muscle |mŭs′əl| *n.* **1.** Body tissue with fibers that loosen or tighten to move parts of the body: *a strong muscle.* **2.** Strength: *enough muscle for the job.* **muscles, muscled, muscling, muscular**

music |myoo′zĭk| *n.* The art of mixing sounds together in interesting arrangements: *played music.* **musical, musicals, musically, musician**

musical |myoo′zĭ kəl| *adj.* Accompanied by music: *a musical act. n.* A musical comedy: *saw the musical.* [see *music*]

mystery |mĭs′tə rē| *adj.* Of or related to a mystery: *mystery books. n.* **1.** A novel or story about a strange event that is not explained until the end: *will read a mystery.* **2.** Something that is unexplained or not understood: *the mystery of black holes.* **mysteries, mysterious, mysteriously**

N

natural |năch′ər əl| *adj.* Made by nature: *a natural food.* [see *nature*]

nature |nā′chər| *n.* The world of living things and the outdoors: *enjoys nature.* **natures, natural, naturally, naturalist, naturalness**

necessary |nĕs′ĭ sĕr′ē| *adj.* Needed; essential: *necessary for good health.* **necessarily, necessitate, necessitates, necessitated, necessitating, necessity, necessities**

need |nēd| *v.* To want or lack: *will soon need water.* **needs, needed, needing, needy, needier, neediest, needless, needlessly, needlessness**

needless |nēd′lĭs| *adj.* Unnecessary: *needless worry.* [see *need*]

neglect |nĭ glĕkt′| *n.* An act of giving little attention to: *ruined by neglect.* **neglects, neglected, neglecting, neglectful, neglectfully, negligent, negligence**

neighbor |nā′bər| *n.* A person who lives nearby: *visited the new neighbor.* **neighbors, neighboring, neighborly, neighborhood**

neighboring |nā′bər ĭng| *adj.* Nearby or bordering: *walked to the neighboring town.* [see *neighbor*]

neither |nē′thər| *conj.* A word used to show two negative choices: *neither you nor I. pron.* Not either one: *if neither spoke.*

nerve |nûrv| *n.* Courage: *lost her nerve.* **nerves, nerved, nerving, nervous, nervously, nervousness, nervy, nervier, nerviest**

nickel |nĭk′əl| *n.* A coin worth five cents in the U.S. and Canada: *found a nickel in the street.* **nickels**

niece |nēs| *n.* A daughter of one's brother or sister: *my oldest niece.* **nieces**

noble |nō′bəl| *adj.* Great in character; generous: *a noble act. n.* A person of high rank or title: *a noble of the court.* **nobler, noblest, nobly, nobles, nobility, nobleness**

normal |nôr′məl| *adj.* Usual or typical: *a normal day.* **normally, normalize, normalcy, normality**

notice |nō′tĭs| *n.* **1.** Attention: *showed little notice.* **2.** An important warning or message: *will read the notice. v.* To see or give attention to: *didn't notice your new sweater.* **notices, noticed, noticing, noticeable, noticeably, notable, notably**

nowhere |nō′hwâr′| *n.* Not anywhere: *nowhere to go.*

ă pat / ā pay / â care / ä father / ĕ pet / ē be / ĭ pit / ī pie / î fierce / ŏ pot / ō go / ô paw, for / oi oil / oo book / oo boot / ou out / ŭ cut / û fur / th the / th thin / hw which / zh vision / ə ago, item, pencil, atom, circus

O

obey |ō **bā′**| v. To do what one is told: *will obey the command.* **obeys, obeyed, obeying, obedient, obediently, obedience**

object |əb **jĕkt′**| v. To oppose: *to object to the decision.* —|**ŏb′**jĭkt| n. Anything that can be seen or touched: *the wooden object.* **objects, objected, objecting, objection, objectionable, objectionably**

observation |ŏb′zûr **vā′**shən| adj. Of or related to observation: *an observation post on the mountain.* n. Something seen: *a close observation.* [see *observe*]

observe |əb **zûrv′**| v. To watch or see: *will observe the animals.* **observes, observed, observing, observation, observations, observational, observer, observatory, observant, observable**

obtain |əb **tān′**| v. To get by effort: *can obtain skill.* **obtains, obtained, obtaining, obtainable, obtainer, obtainment**

onion |**ŭn′**yən| adj. Of an onion: *an onion flavor.* n. A strong-smelling vegetable with a bulb, used cooked or raw: *a slice of onion.* **onions**

opera |**ŏp′**ər ə| n. A play in which music, played by an orchestra, is a major part: *enjoyed the opera.* **operas, operatic, operetta**

operate |**ŏp′**ə rāt′| v. 1. To work or function effectively: *won't operate in the heat.* 2. To perform surgery: *will operate on the patient today.* **operates, operated, operating, operation, operations, operational, operator**

operation |ŏp′ə **rā′**shən| n. 1. An action or activity: *a simple operation.* 2. Surgery: *in the hospital for an operation.* [see *operate*]

oppose |ə **pōz′**| v. To be against: *to oppose the ruling.* **opposes, opposed, opposing, opposite, opposites, oppositely, opposition, oppositeness**

opposite |**ŏp′**ə zĭt| adj. As different as possible: *opposite opinions.* [see *oppose*]

organize |**ôr′**gə nīz′| v. 1. To combine into a group: *will organize a tour group.* 2. To arrange in an orderly way: *to organize the papers.* **organizes, organized, organizing, organizer, organization**

otherwise |**ŭ**th′ər wīz′| adv. 1. Under other circumstances: *would have lost otherwise.* 2. Differently: *shown otherwise.* conj. Or else: *otherwise I'll do it.*

overflow |**ō′**vər flō′| v. To spill over: *if the sink will overflow.* **overflows, overflowed, overflowing**

P

pack |păk| v. To put into a bag or container for storing, selling, etc.: *to pack the dishes.* **unpack, unpacks, unpacked, unpacking, unpacker**

paragraph |**păr′**ə grăf′| n. A group of sentences relating to the same idea and forming a division on a page: *wrote a new paragraph.* **paragraphs, paragraphed, paragraphing**

passage |**păs′**ĭj| n. 1. A part of a speech, writing, or musical composition: *selected a passage.* 2. The act of passing: *the passage of cars.* **passages, passaged, passaging, passenger**

patent |**păt′**nt| v. To obtain a legal document claiming sole rights to an invention: *will patent the new machine.* n. A government document that gives someone the sole rights to make or sell an invention for a certain number of years: *the inventor's patent.* **patents, patented, patenting**

pattern |**păt′**ərn| n. A model or guide used to help make something: *used the pattern.* **patterns, patterned, patterning**

pause |pôz| v. To wait or stop for a short time: *didn't pause at the door.* **pauses, paused, pausing**

pave |pāv| v. To cover with pavement: *will pave the driveway.* **paves, paved, paving, pavement, pavements**

pavement |**pāv′**mənt| n. A surface for streets, sidewalks, etc., that consists of concrete, asphalt, or stones: *to spread the pavement.* [see *pave*]

peer |pîr| v. To look closely at; gaze: *to peer at the photograph.* **peers, peered, peering**

percent |pər **sĕnt′**| n. The parts in each hundred; hundredths: *eighty percent correct.* **percents, percentage, percentages**

perform |pər fôrm'| v. To act or do tricks in public: *will perform before an audience.* *performs, performed, performing, performer, performance*

permanent |pûr'mə nənt| adj. Lasting: *a permanent change.* *permanently, permanence, permanency*

permission |pər mĭsh'ən| n. Consent: *gave her permission.* [see *permit*]

permit |pûr mĭt'| v. To allow: *will permit them to go.* *permits, permitted, permitting, permissive, permissively, permissible, permissiveness, permission*

permitted |pər mĭt'tĭd| v. Allowed: *permitted to enter.* [see *permit*]

person |pûr'sən| n. A human being: *a tall person.* *persons, personal, personally, personable, personalize, personality*

personal |pûr'sə nəl| adj. Private or of a person: *his personal library.* [see *person*]

photograph |fō'tə grăf'| n. A picture taken by a camera: *a recent photograph.* *photographs, photographed, photographing, photo, photography, photographer*

pickle |pĭk'əl| n. A cucumber that has been preserved in salt water or vinegar: *a sour pickle.* *pickles, pickled, pickling*

pier |pîr| n. A walkway that extends into the water and is supported by columns: *fished from the pier.* *piers*

pity |pĭt'ē| n. Distress or sorrow for another: *felt pity for the sick child.* *pities, pitied, pitying, pityingly, pitiful, pitifully, piteous, piteously*

plan |plăn| v. To design or think out ahead of time: *will plan a vacation.* *plans, planned, planning, planner*

plank |plăngk| n. A long piece of sawed wood: *will split a plank.* *planks*

planned |plănd| v. Designed or thought out ahead of time: *planned a trip to Mexico.* [see *plan*]

pleasant |plĕz'ənt| adj. **1.** Agreeable: *a pleasant houseguest.* **2.** Delightful; giving pleasure: *a pleasant sound.* *pleasantly, pleasantry, pleasantness*

pleasure |plĕzh'ər| n. Enjoyment or delight: *the pleasure of reading.* *pleasures, pleasured, pleasuring, pleasurable, pleasurably, pleasureful*

pledge |plĕj| v. To promise: *will pledge their loyalty.* n. A formal promise: *honored the pledge.* *pledges, pledged, pledging*

plunge |plŭnj| v. To throw oneself suddenly into water, a place, etc.: *to plunge into darkness.* n. The act of plunging: *a graceful plunge.* *plunges, plunged, plunging, plunger, plungers*

polish |pŏl'ish| n. A substance used to make something shine: *an oily polish.* v. To make something shine: *will polish the table.* *polishes, polished, polishing, polisher*

polite |pə līt'| adj. Showing good manners: *a polite request.* *politely, politeness*

porter |pôr'tər| n. A person who is employed to carry luggage: *called the porter.* *porters*

positive |pŏz'ĭ tĭv| adj. **1.** Showing agreement; approving: *a positive attitude.* **2.** Absolutely certain: *positive of her skill.* *positively, positiveness*

possible |pŏs'ə bəl| adj. Capable of happening: *a possible win.* *impossible, impossibly, impossibility, impossibilities, impossibleness*

post |pōst| n. The mail: *delivered by post.* *posts, posted, posting, postal, postage*

postage |pō'stĭj| n. The amount charged on anything sent by mail: *thirty cents for postage.* **—Postage stamp—**A stamp for sending something by mail. [see *post*]

postpone |pōst pōn'| v. To delay; put off: *will postpone until tomorrow.* *postpones, postponed, postponing, postponement*

poultry |pōl'trē| adj. Of or related to poultry: *a poultry dinner.* n. Birds such as chickens, turkeys, etc., used as food: *cooking poultry.*

ă pat / ā pay / â care / ä father / ĕ pet / ē be / ĭ pit / ī pie / î fierce / ŏ pot / ō go / ô paw, for / oi oil / ŏŏ book /
ōō boot / ou out / ŭ cut / û fur / th the / th thin / hw which / zh vision / ə ago, item, pencil, atom, circus
© 1977 by Houghton Mifflin Company. Reprinted by permission from THE AMERICAN HERITAGE SCHOOL DICTIONARY.

power |pou'ər| *n.* Force or strength: *the machine's power.* ***powers, powered, powering, powerful, powerfully, powerfulness, powerless, powerlessly, powerlessness***

powerful |pou'ər fəl| *adj.* Strong or forceful: *a powerful athlete.* [see *power*]

practical |prăk'tĭ kəl| *adj.* Useful: *practical advice.* [see *practice*]

practice |prăk'tĭs| *v.* To do something over and over again for improvement: *to practice his singing.* *n.* The action repeated many times to improve a skill: *long hours of practice.* ***practices, practiced, practicing, practical, practically, practicality, practicalness***

prepare |prĭ pâr'| *v.* To make ready for a certain purpose, event, etc.: *will prepare the speech.* ***prepares, prepared, preparing, preparatory, preparedly, preparedness, preparation, preparations***

present |prĭ zĕnt'| *v.* 1. To give: *to present the grand prize.* 2. To offer for thought or consideration: *to present the problem.* ***presents, presented, presenting, presentable, presentably, presently, presentation***

presented |prĭ zĕn'tĭd| *v.* 1. Gave: *presented the check.* 2. Offered for thought or consideration: *presented for discussion.* [see *present*]

prevent |prĭ vĕnt'| *v.* To keep from occurring: *might prevent a fire.* ***prevents, prevented, preventing, preventable, preventative, preventive, preventiveness, prevention***

primary |prī'mĕr'ē| *adj.* First in order or importance: *a primary issue.* —**Primary color**—A color belonging to a group that produces all other colors when mixed together. [see *prime*]

prime |prīm| *adj.* The first in importance: *a prime reason.* ***primes, primed, priming, primer, primarily, primely, primary, primaries***

prison |prĭz'ən| *n.* 1. A building where criminals are housed: *sentenced to a prison.* 2. A place where one is kept against one's will: *if the room became a prison.* ***prisons, prisoner, prisoners***

prisoner |prĭz'ə nər| *n.* 1. A person held unwillingly: *kept as a prisoner.* 2. A person under arrest or in jail: *guarded the prisoner.* —**Prisoner of war**—A person taken by the enemy in wartime. [see *prison*]

private |prī'vĭt| *adj.* Not for public use: *a private path.* ***privates, privately, privacy***

proceed |prə sēd'| *v.* 1. To move forward after having stopped: *will proceed on the trail.* 2. To continue; carry on some action: *will proceed to speak.* ***proceeds, proceeded, proceeding, procedural, procedure***

produce |prə doos'| *v.* 1. To make: *to produce cars.* 2. To bring forth: *will produce fruit.* ***produces, produced, producing, producible, productive, productively, product, production, productivity, producer***

profit |prŏf'ĭt| *v.* To benefit or gain: *will profit from the sale.* *n.* The financial gain made from a business: *a day's profit.* ***profits, profited, profiting, profitable, profitably***

project |prŏj'ĕkt'| *n.* A special assignment carried out by students: *a special history project.* ***projects, projected, projecting, projector***

proof |proof| *n.* A way of showing beyond a doubt the truth of something: *pictures as proof.* [see *prove*]

proper |prŏp'ər| *adj.* Correct: *proper speech.* ***properly***

properly |prŏp'ər lē| *adv.* Correctly: *properly done.* [see *proper*]

prove |proov| *v.* To show the truth of something: *hard to prove his story.* ***proves, proved, proving, proven, proof***

provide |prə vīd'| *v.* To supply what is needed: *will provide a home.* ***provides, provided, providing, provision, provisions, provider***

provisions |prə vĭzh'ənz| *n.* Food supplies: *provisions for the voyage.* [see *provide*]

publish |pŭb'lĭsh| *v.* To print matter for sale or distribution: *will publish the novel.* ***publishes, published, publishing, publisher, publication***

punctual |pŭngk'choo əl| *adj.* On time: *a punctual arrival.* **punctually, punctualness**

punish |pŭn'ĭsh| *v.* To cause pain or discomfort for some wrongdoing: *to punish the known thief.* **punishes, punished, punishing, punishable, punisher, punishment**

purchase |pûr'chĭs| *v.* To buy: *will purchase a house. n.* A buying of something: *a wise purchase.* **purchases, purchased, purchasing, purchaser**

purple |pûr'pəl| *adj.* Of the color purple: *a purple dress. n.* A color made up of a mix of blue and red: *chose purple.* **purples, purpled, purpling, purplish**

purpose |pûr'pəs| *n.* The reason for something: *the purpose of the speech.* **purposes, purposely, purposeful, purposefully, purposefulness, purposeless**

Q

quiet |kwī'ĭt| *adj.* Making little noise: *a quiet library room.* **quiets, quieted, quieting, quieter, quietest, quietly, quietness**

quietly |kwī'ĭt lē| *adv.* Without much noise: *moved quietly.* [see *quiet*]

R

radiate |rā'dē āt'| *v.* To give out rays: *will radiate heat.* **radiates, radiated, radiating, radiant, radiantly, radiance, radiation, radiator**

radiation |rā'dē ā'shən| *n.* The process of giving out rays of heat, light, or other energy: *nuclear radiation.* [see *radiate*]

raid |rād| *n.* A surprise attack: *a midnight raid.* **raids, raided, raiding, raider**

raisin |rā'zən| *n.* A dried grape: *a sweet raisin.* **raisins**

rapid |răp'ĭd| *adj.* Very fast: *a rapid motion.* **rapids, rapidly, rapidness, rapidity**

rapidly |răp'ĭd lē| *adv.* Very quickly: *spoke rapidly.* [see *rapid*]

rascal |răs'kəl| *n.* A mischievous person, especially a child; scamp: *a young rascal.* **rascals, rascally**

rate |rāt| *v.* To judge or grade: *will rate the quality. n.* A class or grade: *third rate.* **rates, rated, rating, ratings, ratio, ration**

rating |rā'tĭng| *v.* Judging or grading: *rating the papers. n.* A position in a class or grade: *a low rating.* [see *rate*]

realize |rē'ə līz'| *v.* To understand fully: *doesn't realize the danger.* **realizes, realized, realizing, realization**

realizes |rē'ə lī'zĭz| *v.* Fully understands: *realizes the problem.* [see *realize*]

receive |rĭ sēv'| *v.* To get: *will receive a package.* **receives, received, receiving, receiver, receipt**

received |rĭ sēvd'| *v.* Got: *received a party invitation.* [see *receive*]

recent |rē'sənt| *adj.* Not long ago: *a recent experience.* **recently, recentness, recency**

reckless |rĕk'lĭs| *adj.* Careless: *a reckless driver.* **recklessly, recklessness**

reduce |rĭ doos'| *v.* To make less or smaller: *to reduce the amount.* **reduces, reduced, reducing, reducible, reducer, reduction**

reflect |rĭ flĕkt'| *v.* To form an image from light that turns back after striking a surface: *will reflect her happy face.* **reflects, reflected, reflecting, reflection, reflections, reflector**

reflection |rĭ flĕk' shən| *n.* A likeness or image formed by light turned back from a surface: *his reflection in the glass.* [see *reflect*]

reform |rĭ fôrm'| *v.* To improve: *to reform the law. n.* A movement or policy to make something better: *a government reform.* **reforms, reformed, reforming, reformer, reformatory, reformation**

refuse |rĭ fyooz'| *v.* To decline; reject: *won't refuse the help.* —|rĕf'yoos| *n.* Waste material; garbage: *to throw out the refuse.* **refuses, refused, refusing, refusal**

ă **pat** / ā **pay** / â **care** / ä **father** / ĕ **pet** / ē **be** / ĭ **pit** / ī **pie** / î **fierce** / ŏ **pot** / ō **go** / ô **paw, for** / oi **oil** / oo **book** / oo **boot** / ou **out** / ŭ **cut** / û **fur** / *th* **the** / th **thin** / hw **which** / zh **vision** / ə **ago, item, pencil, atom, circus**

regard |rĭ gärd′| *n.* Consideration or careful thought: *regard toward others.* **regards, regarded, regarding, regardless, regardlessly**

relate |rĭ lāt′| *v.* To have a connection to: *can't relate one issue to another.* **relates, related, relating, relative, relatives, relatively, relation**

relative |rĕl′ə tĭv| *n.* A person belonging to the same family as another: *a relative of mine.* [see *relate*]

release |rĭ lēs′| *v.* To let go of: *to release its hold. n.* A setting free: *the release of the zoo animals.* **releases, released, releasing**

reliable |rĭ lī′ə bəl| *adj.* Dependable: *a reliable student.* [see *rely*]

rely |rĭ lī′| *v.* To depend on: *can rely on me.* **relies, relied, relying, reliable, reliably, reliability**

represent |rĕp′rĭ zĕnt′| *v.* To speak for: *will represent him in the court trial tomorrow.* **represents, represented, representing, representative, representation**

republic |rĭ pŭb′lĭk| *n.* A government in which citizens elect representatives: *formed a new republic.* **republics, republican**

resolve |rĭ sŏlv′| *v.* To answer and explain: *will resolve the question.* **resolves, resolved, resolving, resolvable, resolution, resolver**

resort |rĭ zôrt′| *n.* A place where people go for recreation: *a beautiful resort.* **resorts, resorted, resorting**

respect |rĭ spĕkt′| *n.* Honor: *respect for the hero.* **respects, respected, respecting, respectful, respectfully, respectable, respectably, respectability**

response |rĭ spŏns′| *n.* An answer: *an excellent response from the student.* **responses, responsible, responsibility**

result |rĭ zŭlt′| *n.* A consequence or outcome: *the test result.* **results, resulted, resulting**

retreat |rĭ trēt′| *v.* To withdraw from: *to retreat from the fire. n.* A withdrawing from an enemy attack: *a sudden retreat.* **retreats, retreated, retreating**

reverse |rĭ vûrs′| *v.* **1.** To change to the opposite: *will reverse our position on the issue.* **2.** To turn in an opposite direction: *to reverse the car.* **reverses, reversed, reversing, reversible, reversibility, reversely, reversal**

rinse |rĭns| *v.* To wash only lightly: *will rinse the cups.* **rinses, rinsed, rinsing**

rot |rŏt| *v.* To spoil or decay: *will rot in the heat.* **rots, rotted, rotting, rotten, rottener, rottenest, rottenly, rottenness**

rotten |rŏt′n| *adj.* Spoiled or decayed: *a rotten banana.* [see *rot*]

rudder |rŭd′ər| *n.* A plate of wood or metal attached to the back of a boat to help steer it: *the sailboat's rudder.* **rudders**

rude |rōōd| *adj.* **1.** Roughly made: *a rude model.* **2.** Impolite: *a rude customer.* **ruder, rudest, rudely, rudeness**

runaway |rŭn′ə wā′| *adj.* Out of control: *a runaway carriage. n.* A person or thing that runs away: *chased the runaway.* **runaways**

S

salad |săl′əd| *n.* A mixture of vegetables: *a delicious salad.* **salads**

salesperson |sālz′pûr′sən| *n.* A person who sells for a living: *a helpful salesperson.* **salespeople**

salute |sə lōōt′| *v.* To show respect by a certain gesture: *to salute the officer.* **salutes, saluted, saluting, saluter, salutation**

sandwich |sănd′wĭch| *n.* Two or more slices of bread with meat or filling between them: *a delicious sandwich.* **sandwiches, sandwiched, sandwiching**

satisfied |săt′ĭs fīd′| *adj.* Pleased: *a satisfied worker. v.* Put an end to: *satisfied their thirst.* [see *satisfy*]

satisfy |săt′ĭs fī′| *v.* **1.** To please: *to satisfy his parents.* **2.** To put an end to: *to satisfy my curiosity:* **satisfies, satisfied, satisfying, satisfyingly, satisfactory, satisfactorily, satisfaction**

scarce |skârs| *adj.* Not enough to meet a demand: *a scarce amount of water.* **scarcer, scarcest, scarcely, scarceness, scarcity**

scarcely |skârs′lē| *adv.* Barely: *scarcely able to finish.* [see *scarce*]

scatter |skăt′ər| *v.* To sprinkle; throw here and there: *will scatter the crumbs.* **scatters, scattered, scattering**

scene |sēn| *n.* **1.** The place where something happened: *scene of the accident.* **2.** A view: *the scene from the window.* **scenes, scenic, scenery**

scissors |sĭz′ərz| *n.* An instrument with two blades for cutting: *trimmed with the scissors.*

scramble |skrăm′bəl| *v.* To crawl or climb: *to scramble over the rocks.* **scrambles, scrambled, scrambling, scrambler**

scratch |skrăch| *v.* **1.** To rub to relieve itching: *to scratch his insect bite.* **2.** To mark or cut with something sharp: *won't scratch the wood.* **scratches, scratched, scratching, scratchy, scratchier, scratchiest, scratchiness, scratcher**

screwdriver |skrōō′drī′vər| *n.* A tool that tightens or loosens screws by turning: *used a drill and a screwdriver to fix the shelf.* **screwdrivers**

search |sûrch| *v.* To look over carefully in order to find something lost or hidden: *to search in the house.* *n.* The act of looking for something: *a careful search.* **searches, searched, searching, searchingly, searcher**

seldom |sĕl′dəm| *adv.* Rarely: *seldom happy.* **seldomly**

select |sĭ lĕkt′| *v.* To choose: *will select a partner.* **selects, selected, selecting, selective, selectively, selectness, selection, selections**

selection |sĭ lĕk′shən| *n.* **1.** A group of people or things chosen to be representative, or a sample: *a selection of shoes.* **2.** A choice: *an excellent selection of books and magazines.* [see *select*]

selfish |sĕl′fĭsh| *adj.* Showing concern only for oneself: *a selfish act.* **selfishly, selfishness**

senior |sēn′yər| *n.* A student in the graduating class of a high school or college: *gave congratulations to the senior. adj.* Older: *a senior member.* **seniors, seniority**

separate |sĕp′ər ĭt′| *adj.* Divided: *separate rooms.* —|sĕp′ə rāt′| *v.* To divide or keep apart: *to separate the group.* **separates, separated, separating, separately, separable, separator, separateness, separation**

serious |sîr′ē əs| *adj.* Thoughtful or grave: *a serious mood.* **seriously, seriousness**

servant |sûr′vənt| *n.* A person hired to work in someone else's household: *employed a servant.* [see *serve*]

serve |sûrv| *n.* The putting of a ball in play by hitting it, as in tennis: *a strong serve. v.* **1.** To work for: *to serve the family loyally.* **2.** To present food to others: *to serve lunch.* **serves, served, serving, server, servant, servants, service**

settle |sĕt′l| *v.* To establish a colony: *to settle in America.* **settles, settled, settling, settler, settlement, settlements**

settlement |sĕt′l mənt| *n.* A colony: *a British settlement.* [see *settle*]

several |sĕv′ər əl| *adj.* Some or few: *several questions.*

severe |sə vîr′| *adj.* Harsh: *severe conditions.* **severer, severest, severely, severity, severeness**

sheriff |shĕr′ĭf| *n.* The chief law-enforcing officer of a county: *elected a sheriff.* **sheriffs**

shoulder |shōl′dər| *n.* The part of the body between the neck and upper arm: *scratched his shoulder.* **shoulders, shouldered, shouldering**

sick |sĭk| *adj.* Ill; not healthy: *was feeling sick.* **sicker, sickest, sickly, sicken, sickens, sickened, sickening, sickeningly**

sicken |sĭk′ən| *v.* To make or become ill: *might sicken the viewer.* [see *sick*]

ă **pat** / ā **pay** / â **care** / ä **father** / ĕ **pet** / ē **be** / ĭ **pit** / ī **pie** / î **fierce** / ŏ **pot** / ō **go** / ô **paw, for** / oi **oil** / ŏŏ **book** / ōō **boot** / ou **out** / ŭ **cut** / û **fur** / *th* **the** / th **thin** / hw **which** / zh **vision** / ə **ago, item, pencil, atom, circus**
©1977 by Houghton Mifflin Company. Reprinted by permission from THE AMERICAN HERITAGE SCHOOL DICTIONARY.

silent |sī′lənt| *adj.* Without speech: *a silent classroom.* ***silently, silence, silences, silenced, silencing, silencer***

simple |sĭm′pəl| *adj.* Plain; easy: *a simple task.* ***simpler, simplest, simplify, simplifies, simplified, simplifying, simplicity, simply***

simply |sĭm′plē| *adv.* Plainly; easily: *simply written.* [see *simple*]

skeleton |skĕl′ĭ tən| *adj.* Relating to a skeleton: *skeleton structure. n.* The supporting structure of bones in the body that protects tissues, muscles, etc.: *examined the skeleton.* ***skeletons, skeletal***

slight |slīt| *adj.* Not much; little: *a slight fever.* ***slights, slighted, slighting, slighter, slightest, slightly, slightness***

slip |slĭp| *v.* To put on or take off easily: *will slip on a blouse.* ***slips, slipped, slipping, slipper, slippers, slippery, slipperiness***

slippers |slĭp′ərz| *n.* Light shoes that can be slipped on and off easily: *a robe and slippers.* [see *slip*]

slither |slĭ*th*′ər| *v.* To move with a sliding motion: *to slither along the floor.* ***slithers, slithered, slithering, slithery***

sole |sōl| *n.* The bottom part of a shoe, boot, etc.: *replaced the sole.* ***soles, soled, soling***

solo |sō′lō| *adj.* Alone; without a partner: *a solo performance.* ***solos, soloist***

solve |sŏlv| *v.* To explain: *will solve the problem.* ***solves, solved, solving, solvable, solver***

solving |sŏl′vĭng| *v.* Explaining: *solving the riddle.* [see *solve*]

source |sôrs| *n.* **1.** The place or person from which something comes: *a source of information.* **2.** The beginning of a river, stream, etc.: *swam to the source.* ***sources***

spade |spād| *v.* To dig with a spade: *will spade the field. n.* A digging tool that has a long handle and an iron blade which can be pushed down into the ground with one's foot: *a shovel and spade.* ***spades, spaded, spading***

spare |spâr| *adj.* Extra: *spare keys.* ***spares, spared, sparing, sparingly, spareness***

speak |spēk| *v.* To talk: *to speak clearly.* ***speaks, spoke, speaking, spoken, speaker, speakers***

speaker |spē′kər| *n.* A person who is talking: *a timid speaker.* [see *speak*]

special |spĕsh′əl| *adj.* Unusual: *a special yearly event.* ***specials, specialize, specializes, specialized, specializing, specialization, specialty, specialist***

speech |spēch| *n.* A talk, especially one prepared for an audience: *an entertaining speech.* ***speeches, speechless***

spirit |spĭr′ĭt| *n.* Enthusiasm: *full of spirit.* ***spirits, spirited, spiritual, spiritless***

spite |spīt| *n.* Ill will: *due to spite.* **—In spite of—**Despite. ***spites, spited, spiting, spiteful, spitefully, spitefulness***

splendid |splĕn′dĭd| *adj.* Grand; wonderful: *a splendid view.* ***splendidly, splendidness***

spoil |spoil| *v.* To become rotten or unusable: *if the vegetables spoil.* ***spoils, spoiled, spoiling, spoiler***

sprang |sprăng| *v.* Leaped or jumped: *sprang over the fence.* [see *spring*]

spread |sprĕd| *v.* To cover with a thin layer: *will spread the jam. n.* Any soft food which can be spread: *a tasty spread.* ***spreads, spreading, spreader***

spring |sprĭng| *v.* To leap or jump: *to spring up.* ***springs, sprang, sprung, springing, springy, springier, springiest***

sprinkle |sprĭng′kəl| *n.* A light rain: *an afternoon sprinkle.* ***sprinkles, sprinkled, sprinkling, sprinkler***

squash |skwŏsh| *n.* A fruit related to the pumpkin and cucumber: *cooked the yellow squash.* ***squashes, squashed, squashing, squashy, squashier, squashiest, squashiness***

squeeze |skwēz| *v.* **1.** To force one's way through something: *to squeeze through the tiny opening.* **2.** To grip: *to squeeze your hand.* ***squeezes, squeezed, squeezing, squeezable, squeezer***

staff |stăf| *n.* A group of employees: *a memo to the staff.* ***staffs, staffed, staffing***

standard |stăn′dərd| *adj.* Normal or accepted size, amount, quality, etc.: *a standard cost.* *n.* A model or basis of comparison: *a standard of excellence.* **standards**

stare |stâr| *v.* To look long and directly at someone or something: *will stare at the mirror.* **stares, stared, staring**

starve |stärv| *v.* To die due to hunger: *if the dog should starve.* **starves, starved, starving, starvation**

stationary |stā′shə nĕr′ē| *adj.* Not moving: *stationary traffic.*

statue |stăch′oo| *n.* An image of someone or something that is formed out of wood, stone, clay, etc.: *a famous statue.* **statues, statuette**

steady |stĕd′ē| *adj.* **1.** Firm; not shaking: *a steady balance.* **2.** Regular: *a steady client.* **steadies, steadied, steadying, steadier, steadiest, steadily, steadiness**

steer |stîr| *v.* To direct or guide the course of something: *can't steer the bicycle.* **steers, steered, steering, steerer, steerable**

sting |stĭng| *v.* To wound with a sharp organ, such as that of certain insects: *will sting her foot.* **stings, stung, stinging, stinger**

stingy |stĭn′jē| *adj.* Ungenerous: *a stingy contribution.* **stingier, stingiest, stingily, stinginess**

stitch |stĭch| *v.* To sew: *to stitch the shirt.* *n.* A link, knot, or loop made by sewing or knitting: *a tiny stitch.* **stitches, stitched, stitching, stitcher**

stomach |stŭm′ək| *adj.* Related to or of the stomach: *stomach pains.* *n.* The organ in the body which digests food: *a full stomach.* **stomachs**

strange |strānj| *adj.* Unknown: *a strange neighborhood.* **stranger, strangest, strangely, strangeness, strangers**

stranger |strān′jər| *n.* An unknown person: *a stranger at the party.* [see *strange*]

strength |strĕngkth| *n.* Power or force: *the strength of twenty-five people.* **strengths, strengthen, strengthens, strengthened, strengthening, strengthener**

stretch |strĕch| *v.* **1.** To extend to full length: *wants to stretch her arms.* **2.** To cause to last: *will stretch the few supplies.* **stretches, stretched, stretching, stretchy, stretchier, stretchiest, stretchable, stretchiness, stretcher**

strict |strĭkt| *adj.* Stern; harsh: *strict rules.* **stricter, strictest, strictly, strictness**

stroll |strōl| *v.* To walk for pleasure: *may stroll in the park.* *n.* A quiet, pleasurable walk: *a stroll after dinner.* **strolls, strolled, strolling, stroller**

struggle |strŭg′əl| *n.* A great effort: *a struggle to stand.* **struggles, struggled, struggling, struggler**

stupid |stoo′pĭd| *adj.* Not intelligent: *a stupid look.* **stupider, stupidest, stupidly, stupidity**

style |stīl| *n.* Fashion: *a particular style.* **styles, styled, styling, stylish, stylishly, stylishness, stylist, styler**

stylish |stī′lĭsh| *adj.* Fashionable: *a stylish dress.* [see *style*]

subject |sŭb′jĭkt| *n.* **1.** In grammar, a word or words about which something is said: *subject and verb.* **2.** A topic: *historical subject.* —|səb jĕkt′| *v.* To cause to experience: *may subject to testing.* **subjects, subjected, subjecting**

submarine |sŭb′mə rēn′| *n.* A ship that can go underwater: *a nuclear submarine.* **submarines**

submit |səb mĭt′| *v.* **1.** To make available; offer: *to submit the paper to the teacher.* **2.** To give up; surrender: *will submit to the winners.* **submits, submitted, submitting**

succeed |sək sēd′| *v.* To do well: *to succeed in high school.* **succeeds, succeeded, succeeding, success, successful, successfully, successfulness**

ă **pat** / ā **pay** / â **care** / ä **father** / ĕ **pet** / ē **be** / ĭ **pit** / ī **pie** / î **fierce** / ŏ **pot** / ō **go** / ô **paw, for** / oi **oil** / oo **book** / oo **boot** / ou **out** / ŭ **cut** / û **fur** / *th* **the** / th **thin** / hw **which** / zh **vision** / ə **ago, item, pencil, atom, circus**
© 1977 by Houghton Mifflin Company. Reprinted by permission from THE AMERICAN HERITAGE SCHOOL DICTIONARY.

sudden |sŭd'n| *adj.* Unexpected: *a sudden noise.* **suddenly, suddenness**

suddenly |sŭd'n lē| *adv.* Unexpectedly: *left suddenly.* [see *sudden*]

suffer |sŭf'ər| *v.* To have pain or grief: *to suffer from a fever.* **suffers, suffered, suffering, sufferer**

suggest |səg jĕst'| *v.* To propose or offer as an idea: *may suggest a movie.* **suggests, suggested, suggesting, suggestive, suggestion, suggestions**

suit |sōot| *v.* To be appropriate for: *to suit their needs.* **suits, suited, suiting, suitable, suitably, suitableness, suitability**

suitable |sōo'tə bəl| *adj.* Proper; appropriate: *a suitable jacket.* [see *suit*]

supply |sə plī'| *n.* A ready-for-use quantity of something: *a large supply of meat.* *v.* To provide what is missing or lacking: *will supply paper and pens.* **supplies, supplied, supplying, supplier**

support |sə pôrt'| *v.* To hold up: *will support the roof.* **supports, supported, supporting, supportive, supportable, supporter**

supreme |sə prēm'| *adj.* The greatest in degree or quality: *supreme happiness.* **supremely, supremeness, supremacy**

surface |sûr'fəs| *n.* The outermost layer of something: *the earth's surface.* *v.* To rise to the top: *if the fish will surface for food.* **surfaces, surfaced, surfacing**

suspect |sə spĕkt'| *v.* **1.** To imagine to be so: *to suspect a trick.* **2.** To believe guilty: *won't suspect those people.* —|sŭs'pĕkt'| *n.* A person thought to have committed a crime: *followed the likely suspect.* **suspects, suspected, suspecting, suspicious, suspiciously, suspicion, suspiciousness**

swift |swĭft| *adj.* Quick or rapid: *a swift current.* **swifter, swiftest, swiftly, swiftness**

swiftly |swĭft'lē| *adv.* Quickly: *walked swiftly.* [see *swift*]

switch |swĭch| *n.* A device used to open or close an electrical circuit: *pressed the switch.* *v.* To exchange: *will switch seats.* **switches, switched, switching, switcher**

system |sĭs'təm| *n.* **1.** A set of parts or elements that work together to form a whole: *an electrical system.* **2.** A plan or method of operation: *my system for studying for a test.* **systems, systematic, systematize**

T

tailor |tā'lər| *n.* A person who sews or mends clothes: *a skillful tailor.* **tailors, tailored, tailoring**

taxi |tăk'sē| *n.* A car for hire with a meter to charge mileage: *will call a taxi.* **taxis, taxied, taxiing**

taxis |tăk'sēz| *n.* More than one taxi: *a line of taxis.* [see *taxi*]

telegraph |tĕl'ə grăf'| *adj.* Of a telegraph: *the telegraph code book.* *n.* A system of communication in which a message is sent by either wire or radio: *received by telegraph.* **telegraphs, telegraphed, telegraphing, telegraphic, telegrapher, telegraphy**

telephone |tĕl'ə fōn'| *n.* An instrument for sending sound or speech at a distance: *dialed the telephone.* **telephones, telephoned, telephoning**

television |tĕl'ə vĭzh'ən| *adj.* Of television: *a television station.* *n.* A device that receives radio waves or electrical signals and reproduces them on a screen: *a portable color television.* **televisions, televise, televises, televised, televising**

term |tûrm| *n.* A period of time in which something lasts: *spring term at school.* **terms, termed, terming**

terrible |tĕr'ə bəl| *adj.* **1.** Extremely bad: *a terrible headache.* **2.** Dreadful or awful: *a terrible noise.* **terribly, terribleness**

territory |tĕr'ĭ tôr'ē| *n.* **1.** An animal's nesting area: *the lion's territory.* **2.** Region or land: *ruled the territory.* **territories, territorial, territorialize**

terror |tĕr'ər| *n.* Extreme fear: *felt terror in the crowd.* **terrors, terrorize, terrorizes, terrorized, terrorizing, terrorizer, terrorist, terrorism**

theater |thē′ə tər| *n.* A place where plays are performed or movies are shown: *two tickets for the theater.* **theaters, theatrical, theatrics**

thief |thēf| *n.* A person who steals: *arrested the thief.* **thieve, thieves, thieved, thieving, thievish, thievery, theft**

think |thĭngk| *v.* To use the mind: *will think about the problem.* **thinks, thought, thinking, thoughtful, thoughtfully, thoughtfulness, thoughts, thoughtless, thoughtlessly, thoughtlessness**

thirst |thûrst| *n.* A dry feeling in the mouth and throat, caused by the lack of anything to drink: *will satisfy their thirst.* **thirsts, thirsted, thirsting, thirsty, thirstier, thirstiest, thirstily, thirstiness**

thirsty |thûr′stē| *adj.* Feeling thirst, or a need for a drink of something: *a thirsty runner.* [see *thirst*]

thoughtful |thôt′fəl| *adj.* **1.** Thinking; full of thought: *replied with a thoughtful answer.* **2.** Considerate: *a thoughtful gift.* [see *think*]

throne |thrōn| *n.* The chair on which a king, queen, or other person of high rank sits for ceremonies: *a throne of gold.* **thrones**

through |thrōō| *prep.* In one side and out the other: *through the house. adj.* Finished: *is through with the work.*

throw |thrō| *v.* To toss or send through the air: *will throw the basketball.* **—Throw out—**To get rid of. **throws, threw, throwing, thrown, thrower**

thrown |thrōn| *v.* Tossed: *had thrown his hat.* [see *throw*]

Thursday |thûrz′dā′| *n.* The fifth day of the week: *will meet on Thursday.* **Thurs.**

tickle |tĭk′əl| *v.* To touch lightly: *to tickle her toes.* **tickles, tickled, tickling, ticklish, tickler, ticklishness**

tickled |tĭk′əld| *v.* Touched lightly: *tickled until he laughed.* [see *tickle*]

tile |tīl| *n.* A thin piece of plastic, concrete, etc., used to cover floors or roofs: *removed the tile.* **tiles, tiled, tiling**

timid |tĭm′ĭd| *adj.* Shy: *a timid look.* **timidly, timidity, timidness**

total |tōt′l| *adj.* Complete or utter: *total confusion. n.* The full amount or sum: *a total of ten dollars.* **totals, totaled, totaling, totally, totality, totalization**

tour |tŏŏr| *n.* A trip in which several places of interest are seen: *an African tour.* **tours, toured, touring, tourist, tourism**

tournament |tŏŏr′nə mənt| *n.* A series of contests involving one sport: *a tennis tournament.* **tournaments, tourney**

towel |tou′əl| *adj.* For or related to a towel: *a towel bar. n.* A cloth or piece of paper used to dry things that are wet: *a fresh towel.* **towels, toweled, toweling**

traffic |trăf′ĭk| *n.* Cars, people, ships, etc., that are traveling at a particular time: *traffic on the highway.*

transport |trăns pôrt′| *v.* To carry from one place to another: *to transport oil.* **transports, transported, transporting, transporter, transportation, transportable**

transportation |trăns′pər tā′shən| *n.* The means, such as a bus, train, etc., of going from one place to another: *depends on reliable transportation.* [see *transport*]

travel |trăv′əl| *v.* To go from one place to another: *will travel on a business trip.* **travels, traveled, traveling, traveler, travelers**

traveler |trăv′ə lər| *n.* A person who goes from one place to another: *a lonely traveler.* [see *travel*]

treat |trēt| *v.* **1.** To behave toward: *to treat unfairly.* **2.** To try to help or cure with some remedy: *will treat the disease.* **treats, treated, treating, treatable, treatment, treatments**

ă pat / ā pay / â care / ä father / ĕ pet / ē be / ĭ pit / ī pie / î fierce / ŏ pot / ō go / ô paw, for / oi oil / ŏŏ book / ōō boot / ou out / ŭ cut / û fur / th the / th thin / hw which / zh vision / ə ago, item, pencil, atom, circus
©1977 by Houghton Mifflin Company. Reprinted by permission from THE AMERICAN HERITAGE SCHOOL DICTIONARY.

treatment |trēt′mənt| *n.* **1.** Behavior toward something: *kind treatment.* **2.** Something done or used to create relief; a cure: *medical treatment.* [see *treat*]

treaty |trē′tē| *n.* A formal written agreement between nations or states that includes terms of peace, trade, etc.: *agreed to make a treaty.* **treaties**

trial |trī′əl| *n.* **1.** A test of something to check its quality, strength, fitness, etc.: *tested as a trial.* **2.** An effort: *a trial to finish.* **trials**

trim |trim| *v.* To neaten by removing parts not needed: *will trim the branches.* **trims, trimmed, trimming, trimmer, trimmest, trimness**

trimmed |trimd| *v.* Neatened by removing parts not needed: *trimmed her hair.* [see *trim*]

truth |trōōth| *n.* The actual state of affairs: *spoke only the truth.* **truths, truthful, truthfully, truthfulness**

truthful |trōōth′fəl| *adj.* Honest: *a truthful witness.* [see *truth*]

twilight |twī′līt′| *adj.* Of or related to twilight: *the twilight hours. n.* The faint light in the sky before the sun rises and after it sets: *will leave at twilight.* **twilights**

twist |twĭst| *v.* To turn or wind: *to twist the rope.* **twists, twisted, twisting, twister**

typewrite |tīp′rīt′| *v.* To write with a typewriter: *will typewrite a memo.* **typewrites, typewrote, typewritten, typewriting, typewriter, typewriters**

typewriter |tīp′rī′tər| *n.* A machine for writing, which makes letters look like print: *an office typewriter.* [see *typewrite*]

U

umpire |ŭm′pīr′| *n.* The person who rules on the plays in a game: *signal from the umpire.* **umpires, umpired, umpiring**

uncertain |ŭn sûr′tn| *adj.* **1.** Apt to change: *uncertain forecast.* **2.** Unsure or doubtful: *uncertain about the facts.* [see *certain*]

uneasy |ŭn ē′zē| *adj.* Nervous or restless: *uneasy behavior.* [see *easy*]

union |yōōn′yən| *n.* A group of workers united together to protect their interests: *belongs to the union. adj.* Of or related to a union: *union wages.* **unions, unionize, unionizes, unionized, unionizing**

unjust |ŭn jŭst′| *adj.* Not fair: *an unjust rule.* [see *just*]

unpack |ŭn păk′| *v.* To remove items packed in a suitcase, box, etc.: *will unpack the trunk.* [see *pack*]

unwise |ŭn wīz′| *adj.* Foolish: *an unwise choice.* [see *wise*]

use |yōōz| *v.* To put into service: *will use the machine.* **uses, used, using, useful, usefully, usefulness, useless, uselessly, uselessness**

useless |yōōs′lĭs| *adj.* Not able to be used: *a useless tool.* [see *use*]

V

vacant |vā′kənt| *adj.* Empty: *a vacant room.* **vacantly, vacate, vacates, vacated, vacating, vacantness, vacancy**

vain |vān| *adj.* Overly prideful about one's appearance or abilities: *a vain and proud mayor.* **—In vain—**Without success. **vainly, vainness, vanity, vanities**

valuable |văl′yōō ə bəl| *adj.* Worth a lot of money: *a valuable necklace.* [see *value*]

value |văl′yōō| *n.* The worth or price of something: *of tremendous value.* **values, valued, valuing, valuably, valueless, valuate, valuable, valuables, valuation**

vanish |văn′ĭsh| *v.* To disappear suddenly: *to vanish from view.* **vanishes, vanished, vanishing**

vanity |văn′ĭ tē| *n.* Too much pride; boasting: *showed much vanity.* **—Vanity plate—**A special license plate made up of letters or numbers particularly requested by an owner of a car, truck, etc. [see *vain*]

various |vâr′ē əs| *adj.* Different: *various conclusions.* [see *vary*]

vary |vâr′ē| *v.* To make different: *to vary the menu.* **varies, varied, varying, various, variously, variety**

vegetable |vĕj′tə bəl| *n.* A plant whose seeds, leaves, roots, and fruit are used for food: *a crisp vegetable.* **vegetables**

velvet |vĕl′vĭt| *adj.* Of velvet: *a velvet hat.* *n.* Soft, thick cloth made of rayon, silk, nylon, etc.: *a dress of velvet.* **velvets, velvety**

vice |vīs| *n.* A bad habit: *gave up his one vice.* **vices, vicious, viciously, viciousness**

victory |vĭk′tə rē| *n.* Triumph or success in a contest: *an unexpected victory.* **victories, victorious, victoriously, victoriousness, victor**

volcano |vŏl kā′nō| *n.* A hill or mountain built from the ash and lava that have erupted from the earth's crust: *an active volcano.* **volcanoes, volcanic**

volume |vŏl′yoom| *n.* **1.** Amount: *a tremendous volume of paper.* **2.** Loudness: *will turn down the volume.* **3.** One book from a set of books: *the sixth volume.* **volumes**

voyage |voi′ĭj| *n.* A long journey: *a sea voyage.* **voyages, voyaged, voyaging, voyager**

vulgar |vŭl′gər| *adj.* Showing lack of taste or manners: *a vulgar laugh.* **vulgarly, vulgarity**

W

wander |wŏn′dər| *v.* To travel here and there without purpose: *may wander for several hours.* **wanders, wandered, wandering, wanderer**

warehouse |wâr′hous′| *n.* A building where goods are stored: *kept at the warehouse.* **warehouses**

wealth |wĕlth| *n.* Riches or property: *inherited wealth.* **wealthy, wealthier, wealthiest, wealthily, wealthiness**

weave |wēv| *v.* To make a finished product by interlacing threads: *will weave a blanket.* **weaves, weaved, weaving, wove, woven, weaver**

week |wēk| *n.* Seven days: *absent for a week.* **weeks, weekly**

weekly |wēk′lē| *adj.* Once each week: *a weekly meeting.* [see *week*]

weight |wāt| *n.* How heavy something is: *height and weight.* **weights, weighty, weigh, weighs, weighed, weighing, weightless, weightlessness, weigher**

whether |wĕth′ər| *conj.* A word that expresses a choice or an alternative: *whether we continue.*

whisper |wĭs′pər| *n.* A soft, low tone of voice: *to speak in a whisper.* **whispers, whispered, whispering**

whistle |wĭs′əl| *n.* A high-pitched sound: *a loud whistle.* **whistles, whistled, whistling, whistler**

width |wĭdth| *n.* The distance across something: *a width of ten feet.* **widths**

wise |wīz| *adj.* Showing good sense; smart: *a wise decision.* **unwise, unwisely**

wool |wool| *n.* The soft fur of sheep: *a coat made of wool.* **wools, wooly, woolier, wooliest, woolen, woolens**

woolen |wool′ən| *adj.* Made from wool: *woolen socks.* [see *wool*]

wrap |răp| *v.* **1.** To cover something by folding and tying paper around it: *will wrap the book.* **2.** To wind around: *will wrap the string around it.* **wraps, wrapped, wrapping, wrapper**

wrapped |răpt| *v.* **1.** Covered with paper and tied: *wrapped the package.* **2.** To draw or wind around: *wrapped the blanket around her.* [see *wrap*]

wrench |rĕnch| *n.* A tool for turning bolts and nuts: *used a heavy wrench.* **wrenches, wrenched, wrenching**

ă pat / ā pay / â care / ä father / ĕ pet / ē be / ĭ pit / ī pie / î fierce / ŏ pot / ō go / ô paw, for / oi oil / oo book /
oo boot / ou out / ŭ cut / û fur / th the / th thin / hw which / zh vision / ə ago, item, pencil, atom, circus
©1977 by Houghton Mifflin Company. Reprinted by permission from THE AMERICAN HERITAGE SCHOOL DICTIONARY.